CASTLES

of the

MARCHES

CASTLES
of the
MARCHES

JOHN KINROSS

AMBERLEY

This edition first published 2015

Amberley Publishing
The Hill, Stroud
Gloucestershire GL5 4EP

www.amberley-books.com

British Library Cataloguing in Publication Data.
A catalogue record for this book is available from the British Library.

ISBN 978 1 4456 4800 2 (print)
ISBN 978 1 4456 4801 9 (ebook)

Typesetting and Origination by Amberley Publishing.
Printed in Great Britain.

CONTENTS

Acknowledgements

Thanks to Christopher Thompson for organising the illustrations – and taking some of the photographs – Bernard Lowry for introducing me to some of the North Shropshire castles and taking photographs, and to my son Alastair and my brother-in-law William for others. Special thank-yous go to my wife for her patience, to Sallyann who prepared the text for the publishers and Alison Poole who drew some key plans.

JSK
Hereford, 2015

INTRODUCTION

Castles are a Norman invention, but the Englishman's home as we all know is his castle. The Saxons had developed motte and bailey castles of earth and wood palisades. Those who lived in them must have soon realised how uncomfortable they were. The Normans arrived and the defensive fortress was built of stone with a central keep, usually taller than other towers, and walled baileys with surrounding moats or dry ditches became the norm. Most have chapels, kitchens and elaborate entrances. Some, like Goodrich, have barbicans.

Rectangular keeps often had insufficient room so shell-keeps on the bailey wall as at Huntington were constructed. The castles at Hereford and Ludlow used the town walls as extra defences. Inside the bailey were stables for horses, a chapel, granary, well and sundry buildings for farming purposes. The solar was the comfortable part of the castle where the lord and his family lived. The garrison had a guardroom and quarters in other parts of the castle. At White Castle, the outer bailey had enough space for a passing army to bivouac inside the castle walls.

The rise of the Mortimers of Wigmore contributed to the Yorkist victories in the Wars of the Roses. King Edward IV, victor of the Battle of Mortimer's Cross (1461) and of Tewkesbury (1471) was a Plantagenet but his grandmother was a Mortimer and he was the 7th Earl of March as well as King of England between 1461 and 1483. The Council of the Marches began as the 'Prince's Council' but it developed into a strong arm of local government with a Lord President, Secretary, Clerk, Clerk of the Signet, Attorney, Solicitor, Porter and Sergeant of Arms. It dealt with all criminals, local militia, civil titles, debts, enclosures, supervising JPs and many other matters. It was suspended during the Civil War but restored at the Restoration (1660) and was only finally ended by King William III due to corruption charges and to the desire of William and Mary to keep governmental control centred in London.

Thus the Welsh risings of Owain Glyndwr and Llewelyn were kept in check by the Marcher Lords and the castles built by King Edward I and later kings. Today we see the remains of these castles, some very overgrown, others in reasonable condition – Ludlow and Goodrich – one restored and lived-in (Pembridge) and others fortified manor houses like Upton Cresset that have been repaired over the years and are well worth a visit. The main castles, Ludlow and Goodrich, have impressive remains, which is one of the reasons for writing this book. An early tourist with a camera was young Fletcher Moss, who cycled around the border in 1901 with a friend and visited Albright Hussey, Caus, Myddle Castle, Goodrich and Treago. I have included some of his photographs. Fletcher and his friend were charged eightpence per person when they visited Ludlow Castle and had to argue with the man at the gate for their change. The latter wanted an extra fourpence for their bicycles parked in the courtyard. After an argument the man, 'who would rather part with his teeth than his money', let them through with their precious camera.

John Kinross, Hereford
January 2015

KEY

CADW   Welsh Historic Monuments
EHT   English Heritage Trust
NT   National Trust

LIST OF CASTLES

HEREFORDSHIRE CASTLES

Almeley
Ashperton
Bacton
Bosbury
Brampton Bryan
Bredwardine
Breinton
Bronsil
Byton
Castle Frome
Clifford
Croft
Cublington
Cusop
Dilwyn
Dorstone
Eardisley
Ewyas Harold
Goodrich
Hampton Court
Hereford
Huntington
Kentchurch
Kilpeck

Kingsland
Kington
Kinnersley
Lingen
Longtown
L. Brockhampton
Lyonshall
Moccas
Monnington Court
Much Marcle
Old Castleton
Pembridge
Penyard
Richard's Castle
Snodhill
Stapleton (Presteigne)
Staunton-on-Arrow
Tretire
Treago
Urishay
Weobley
Wigmore
Wilton

SHROPSHIRE CASTLES

Acton Burnell
Alberbury
Albright Hussey
Apley
Bishop's Castle
Bridgnorth
Brockhurst
Broncroft
Burford (nr Tenbury)
Castle Pulverbatch
Caus
Charlton
Cheney Longville
Clun
Corfham
Ellesmere
High Ercall
Holdgate
Hopton
Knockin
Langley Hall
Ludlow
More
Moreton Corbet
Myddle
Oswestry
Quatford
Red Castle
Rowton
Ryton
Shrawardine
Shrewsbury
Stapleton (Salop)
Stokesay
Tong
Upton Cresset
Wattleborough
Wem
Whitchurch
Whittington

WELSH BORDERS

Brecon
Chepstow
Hay-on-Wye
Montgomery
Monmouth

THE THREE CASTLES

Grosmont
Skenfrith
White Castle

FOREST OF DEAN

St Briavels

CHESHIRE

Aldford
Beeston
Chester
Doddington
Doddleston
Dunham Massey
Frodsham
Halton
Macclesfield
Malpas
Pulford
Shipbrook
Shocklach
Shotwick
Stockport

NORTH WALES

Chirk
Denbigh
Flint
Rhuddlan

HEREFORDSHIRE CASTLES

1. ALMELEY CASTLE

Only a few mounds remain close to Almeley church of the home of Sir John Oldcastle. He was a wit, a poet and a soldier who joined the Lollard sect. A drinking friend of young Prince Hal, Shakespeare used him as an inspiration for his character Falstaff, but he was arrested for treason in Guilsfield, Montgomeryshire and taken to London where he was burnt at the stake on Christmas Day 1417.

The castle passed to the Crown and was restored to the family of Milbourne, descendants of the Oldcastles, and in the seventeenth century it is recorded as the property of Thomas Monnington of Sarnesfield.

2. ASHPERTON CASTLE

Close to Ledbury, Ashperton Castle was the property of William de Grandison who married the wealthy heiress of John de Tregoz (the Tregoz family tombs are in Foy church on the banks of the Wye). He obtained a licence to crenellate his house at Ashperton. Their son, John de Grandison, was Bishop of Exeter for a record forty-two years and was known as the 'Stout Stomach'. The Bishop's elder brother, Sir Peter, was a member of King Edward III's parliament and his younger brother, Sir Otho, was ambassador to the Pope. The castle has vanished but most of the moat remains. The church is inside the outer bailey.

3. BACTON

A small castle was built by William de Bacton at Newcourt Farm in the Golden Valley. It had a triangular court and a round keep. Bacton church is famous for the memorial of Blanche Parry, a leading maid to Queen Elizabeth I. She died a maid too as her inscription says:

A maede in Courte and never no man's wyffe
Sworne of Quene Ellsbeths hedd chamber allwaye
Wy the maedeb Quene a maede dyd ende my lyffe.

4. BOSBURY PALACE

Close to the church and next to Moreton's Grammar School are the gates of the Bishop's Palace dating from the fourteenth century. It was moated and belonged to the Bishops of Hereford. Here Bishop Athelstan died, and Bishop Swinfield also died in 1316. It was rebuilt in 1572 and was restored after the Civil War becoming a farmhouse.

5. BRAMPTON BRYAN

The considerable remains of Brampton Bryan Castle are in the grounds of the Hall, which was built for Sir Edward Harley in 1661. The castle was built by Barnard Unspec, Lord of Brampton in the reign of King Henry I, and passed in 1309 to the Harleys when Margaret de Brampton married Edward Harley. In 1293 it was described as a 'tower with cartilage, garden and vivary worth £8.7s 8d.'

The Harleys fought for the Yorkists during the Wars of the Roses and were present at Flodden in Surrey's army that beat the Scots. In 1580 they put up Campion and Parsons, Jesuits, in the castle but in 1631 Sir Robert Harley, a Puritan, was a Parliamentarian and left for London leaving his wife, Lady Brilliana, and a small garrison in the castle. In July 1643 Sir William Vavasour and his Royalist forces decided it was time to capture Brampton Bryan with his artillery – Lady Harley had only two drakes but enough powder, and shot for a two-month siege. After seven weeks, the Royalists left to go to help the king's army at Gloucester. There were no casualties – except the cook, who was killed by a poisoned bullet – and all her husband's sheep and horses. Most of the village was burnt and Lady Brilliana's last letter to her son at Oxford said she 'was ill with a very greate colde' from which she died. Her docter, Mr Wright, took command of the garrison as another attack was expected, and it came in April 1644 when Sir Michael Woodhouse battered the castle into submission and sent all prisoners to Shrewsbury including three of Lady Harley's children. Sir Robert drew up a 'particular' of his losses after the war and was told to claim it from Sir Henry Lingen, the Royalist governor of Hereford. As he was absent, it was presented to Lady Lingen with the following demand:

Stock of cattle	£940
Loss of £1500 for 3 years	£4,500
The castle itself being utterly ruined	£3,000
All the furniture and household goods	£2,500
Two mills with Brewhouses	£950
A study of books valued at	£200
Two parks wholly laid open and destroyed	£300

1. Brampton Bryan ruin

2. Brampton Bryan

Destroyed at least 500 deer	£1,400
Destroyed more in corn	£100
Total:	£13,890

Edward, Robert's son, then a Parliamentary officer, had a brief answer from Lady Lingen asking if her husband (in prison) had approved it. Edward then waived his right to the demands. His father returned home (he had been Governor of Dunkirk) and, using castle stone wherever possible, built the hall where the family still reside. The hall is open to local groups during the summer. On view are some arms and armour, the castle key and a splendid picture of Lady Brilliana.

6. BREDWARDINE

Bredwardine, between Hereford and Hay, is on the Wye and had a castle with a long bailey and motte defending a ford over the river. It belonged to the Baskerville family but in 1600 the Vaughans built a tower house here, probably more for the view than for the purpose of defence. At the Battle of Agincourt, it was Davy Gam and Roger Vaughan who saved the life of the King when he was pressed by several French knights. They were both killed but were knighted before expiring. Sir Roger's descendants lived at Bredwardine for some time before moving to Moccas. (see page 28). Nothing remains today of their castle but a mound and a few signs of the castle fishponds.

3. Brampton Bryan Gatehouse

7. BREINTON

The treasurer of Hereford Cathedral had a stone house here in medieval times. It was excavated in 1959–62 and some foundations discovered with a north gateway and curtain wall and ditch close to the river. Of great interest in the church is a wooden memorial (in the vestry now) to Captain Rudhall Booth who was the custodian of Lindisfarne Castle and a relation of Bishop Booth. He was a devout Catholic and a soldier of James II's army, but died of a sudden illness when on duty miles from his home in Breinton.

8. BRONSIL

These castle remains are in Eastnor Park near Ledbury and permission to view should be obtained from the land agent at Eastnor (01531 632302) first. Eastnor Castle was built in 1815 for Lord Somers and does not constitute a castle in the terms of this book.

There is a Buck's print of Bronsil in 1731, which shows an early square construction with eight round towers surrounded by a wet moat – this too is surrounded by a dry moat. It was built by the Beauchamp family. Richard, Lord Beauchamp, obtained a licence in 1449 to crenellate his house. After a brief period when it came to the Talbots, it was passed by marriage to the Reeds.

At the end of the sixteenth century, the castle was said to have become haunted by the ghost of the first Lord Beauchamp, and Gabriel Reed consulted a specialist on ghostly apparitions, which meant a journey to Italy as he had died abroad. The ghost vanished but when the Reeds moved to a more comfortable house at Lugwardine they took the bones with them. Gradually, the castle collapsed and the final tower fell as recently as 1991. Perhaps the spirit of the first lord has returned?

4. Bronsil/Brantsil

9. BYTON

Close to the church there is a motte visible with the twin tower remains of a small entrance as at Clifford. No stones are visible above ground. Byton is near Presteigne.

10. CASTLE FROME

The De Lacy family had an eleventh-century castle here, which is now not easy to see due to forestation. It had a large shell keep and the motte is 12 feet high. The surrounding ditch has a southern causeway. Castle Frome church is famous for its Romanesque font carved by the same Hereford School as Kilpeck's carvings; it is well worth a visit.

11. CLIFFORD

One of FitzOsbern's castles, stones still remain of Clifford Castle close to the Wye and near the toll bridge to Hay. At Domesday the castle was granted to Ralph de Tosny whose daughter married Richard Fitz-Pons. They changed their name to Clifford, and Walter Clifford, their son, had a daughter who was known as 'Fair Rosamund', the mistress of King Henry II. Walter was asked to pay off his debts and, according to tradition, the King's messenger who summoned him was asked to 'eat the King's writ, Waxe and all.' The incensed King promptly captured Clifford, which on Walter's death passed to Matilda Clifford, wife of the Earl of

5. Clifford Castle

Salisbury. It still remained in the Clifford family until 1675 when they moved to their more substantial castle at Skipton, Yorkshire. Clifford Castle passed to the Mortimers, the Witneys and, in 1547, to Lord Clinton. It was allowed to decay and today it has several stones remaining but is not open to the public although fairly visible from the road. Mr Robinson said that in 1869 the ruins were saved by Tomkyns Dew and, compared with other ruined castles in the county, Clifford has more than most.

12. CROFT CASTLE

Croft Castle today is a fourteenth- and fifteenth-century building with four round angle towers. It was Gothicised in the eighteenth century and is no longer square in shape. It passed to Richard Knight in 1746 who added to its comfort so that it is difficult to see any form of defence today – no moat, gatehouse or anything to hinder an attacker.

In the chapel next door is the tomb of Sir Richard Croft in armour. He was on the victorious side at the battles of Mortimer's Cross, Tewkesbury and Stoke. He was knighted by King Henry VII at Stoke. One of his descendants was comptroller of Queen Elizabeth's household and during the Civil War another was killed at Stokesay fighting for King Charles I.

In 1923, the Croft family purchased the castle back, but in 1957 it was acquired by the National Trust.

NT. Open February – December, tea room, shop, garden and play area. For more information tel: 01568 782120 or visit croftcastle@nationaltrust.org.uk.

13. CUBLINGTON

The De La Fields had a castle here near Madley at Castle Farm. There are slight remains of a motte and bailey. There used to be a stained-glass image of Sir John de la Field in Madley church in armour at prayer.

14. CUSOP

Close to Hay-on-Wye, Cusop had a castle near the church that belonged to the Clavenogh family. Philip de Clavenogh was a supporter of the Earl of Lancaster in the Baron's War and with others was responsible for the death of Piers Gaveston – a favourite of King Edward II. He was executed by the barons on Blacklow Hill, Warwick, in June 1312. Cusop seems to have been a tower with a surrounding bank and wall and a stone entrance. Robinson says that he knew a woman in 1860 who remembered the stone walls there. On the hill above is a motte and bailey, known for some reason as Mouse Castle that probably belonged to the same family.

15. DILWYN

There is a large circular moated area near the village green and, in the centre, excavation revealed a square keep that was the home of the Gamage family (who still live in Herefordshire today). In the thirteenth century it passed to William de Braose and later was divided between the Mallory and FitzWarin families. There are at least three other moated sites in Dilwyn but this one is the largest.

16. DORSTONE

A large motte and bailey (the motte now tree-covered) covers 2.5 acres close to the village centre. At Domesday it belonged to the Fitz Poyntz family but it passed to the De Sollers family until Henry IV gave it to Sir Walter Fitzwalter in 1403 with orders to strengthen it. The remains of a D-shaped tower may date from then. In 1422 it passed to Richard de la Mare, a hero of Agincourt whose brass (1435), together with that of Isabella his wife, are in the north transept of the cathedral in Hereford. He is in full armour and she is wearing a butterfly headdress.

The Royal Army under Charles I stayed at Dorstone en route for Holme Lacy in 1645 but whether they camped among ruins or whether there was a living area fit for a king we do not know. Finally it became a possession of the Cornewalls.

17. EARDISLEY

The motte and bailey now occupied by Castle Farm behind the church marks the site of Eardisley Castle, home of the Baskervilles. Sir John Baskerville fought as a boy with distinction at Agincourt and his son, Sir James, fought for King Henry VII at the battle of Stoke in 1487, where he was made a Knight Baronet. His wife, Lady Sybil, was the sister of Lord Ferrars who was killed at Bosworth fighting for Richard III. Another Baskerville commanded Queen Elizabeth's army in Picardy, and in the Civil War the Baskervilles were for the king. Alas, a mob from Hereford attacked and burnt their castle so nothing remains apart from the farmhouse, built *c.* 1700.

18. EWYAS HAROLD

Only a large motte and bailey built pre-conquest by Osborne Pentecost and then re-fortified by the builder of Chepstow Castle (see page 62), William FitzOsbern in 1067. Later, a priory was built to the south of the castle by the Benedictines of Gloucester. Later owners were the Tregoz and de la Warre families. At the Battle of Poitiers (1556) it was John Tregoz who captured King John of France. He must have obtained some profit from this but in 1403 we find King Henry IV passing it to Robert de Vache so that it could be strengthened against the army of Owain Glyndwr. It passed eventually to the Nevilles but by the Civil War it was too ruinous to be of any consequence.

19. GOODRICH

Goodrich, close to the Wye, was built to defend the river crossing there and more of it remains today than any of the Herefordshire castles. The builder, in early Norman times, was Godric Mapson but the rectangular keep is supposed to have been built by Richard de Clare (1160). It then passed via his daughter Isabella to her husband William Marshal, Earl of Pembroke. His granddaughter married William de Valence and the castle was rebuilt in William's time with grants of timber and money from the king. The 60-foot-long hall was larger and grander than most castle halls. The gatehouse with its drawbridge and two portcullises was constructed next to the large chapel. (A photograph of the ruined chapel was taken by Fletcher Moss in around 1900 and a drawing of the complete castle chapel at the time of the Talbots can be seen in the guidebook). The barbican was built later with a passage down to the dry moat so that horses could be taken round the castle's west wall where the stable block with its wooden roof was positioned.

From the fourteenth to the fifteenth century, the Talbots lived here in some style – the stair to their private seat overlooking the chapel is still there and the kitchen had running water which rendered the deep well unnecessary. Colonel Lingen and his 200 cavaliers held it during the Civil War. Food and timber was always needed and one of the sufferers was Sir Edward Powell of Pengethley Manor (now a favourite eating place). Annoyed by this, in March 1645 Col Birch (his statue in armour can be seen in Weobley church) set out at night with a force of around fifty Parliamentary horses and fifty musketeers. He must have had inside information on the layout as his men, using ladders, climbed the wall near the stables, let loose some horses and set fire to the stable roof. This setback was a blow for the Royalists as their water supply had been cut and it was not long before Birch returned with his 'Roaring Meg' – a huge mortar (now inside the castle courtyard) and on 31 July 1646, down to his last four barrels of powder, Lingen surrendered, marching out of the castle with his fiddlers playing 'Harry Lingen's March'.

The castle chapel was visited in 1902 by Fletcher Moss and his friend 'X' on their bikes with their camera: 'It was half past seven on a fine but misty evening in June. We bang at the gate ... an amusing old gentleman comes out and says that the charge would be a guinea for professionals (photographer) or 1s for amateurs. My first thought is to throw him in the moat and take the castle but on second thoughts we give him 2s.' Photographs are taken, walls are scrambled up and three altars are examined before they remount their bikes they often recross the bridge and make for Walford.

In 1942, a Halifax bomber belonging to the Royal Radar establishment in Malvern crashed near the castle and eleven men were killed. There is a monument there in the form of a stained-glass chapel window erected in their memory. One of them (Flying Officer A. M. Phillips, died at Goodrich on 7 June, 1942) is also remembered on the chapel memorial at my old school. In 2000, the Bishop of Hereford dedicated the large triple-light window to the Wye parishes of Goodrich, Marstow and Welsh Bicknor by Nicky Hopwood. The floor and door have been repaired so the chapel is now usable.

Above: 9. Goodrich Old Gatehouse

Left: 8. Goodrich entrance today

Below: 11. Goodrich Chapel today

Right: 10. Goodrich – Old Chapel

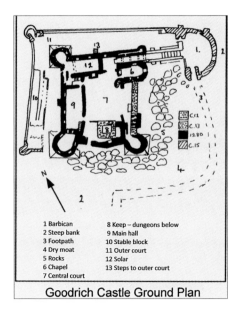

Goodrich Castle Ground Plan

1 Barbican
2 Steep bank
3 Footpath
4 Dry moat
5 Rocks
6 Chapel
7 Central court
8 Keep – dungeons below
9 Main hall
10 Stable block
11 Outer court
12 Solar
13 Steps to outer court

Above: 7. Goodrich plan

Left: 12. Goodrich – Roaring Meg

Below: 13. Hampton Court front

EHT Open (2015) April to September: 10.00 a.m. to 6.00 p.m., October to November: 10.00 a.m. to 5.00 p.m., November to February: Saturday/Sunday 10.00 a.m. to 4.00 p.m. Non-refundable parking charge of £1.00. Tea room and shop closed thirty minutes before castle. Telephone 01600 890538 for further details.

20. HAMPTON COURT

Not to be confused with the building on the Thames, Hampton Court at Hope-under-Dinmore is more of a country house than a castle. Sir Rowland Leinthall obtained a licence to crenellate his house in 1434. His wife, Margaret FitzAlan, was the granddaughter of the Earl of Arundel – a wealthy magnate and a relation of the Royal family. When Sir Rowland died, his daughter married Sir Thomas Cornewall of Burford, Shropshire. In 1510 it passed by marriage to the Coningsbys who had it for three centuries. Thomas Coningsby, a soldier in William of Orange's army, saved the life of his king at the Battle of the Boyne when a cannonball grazed William's shoulder after Thomas had persuaded the royal party to move further away from the river. The bloodstained handkerchief remained with the family for years and Thomas prepared two rooms for the king and queen in 1689 when he expected them to visit him for a weekend. History does not relate what happened but it is thought no such visit took place. After passing to the Arkwrights, it was sold in 1994 to the Van Kampens who are responsible for the large collection of armour. The present owners use it for weddings and the chapel, though small, is probably the finest room in the castle today.

Privately owned, Hampton Court is open during the summer to visitors. For details, go to www.hamptoncourt.org.co, (telephone 01568 79777). The grounds are popular with children and are open when the court is closed.

21. HEREFORD

Before the Normans arrived in 1066, the Anglo-Saxon chronicle reported that 'Foreigners had built a castle in Herefordshire in Earl Swain's territory', presumably meaning Hereford itself. We know that Harold fortified Hereford in 1055 and that there was a castle there by 1067. The walls, of which, like Canterbury, a significant presence remains, were not finished in stone until 1265.

Today, apart from a few lengths of the town wall and the castle green, there is no sign of Hereford Castle, once described by Leland as 'nearly as large as Windsor'. It was built by William FitzOsbern shortly after the Norman invasion. It had two wards, one with a large motte and the rectangular keep inside with four round corner towers and two have circular towers to east and west. The large bailey (now a park) had two defended gatehouses.

The Wye acted as a moat and the town walls as a further defence. A brook provided the water and a mill was also water-driven. Milo the Constable held the castle for Maud but King Stephen transferred the ownership to Robert de Bellamont, Earl of Leicester, who took up arms against the king in the Baron's War. Here came the young Prince Edward as a prisoner after the Battle of Lewes, but Simon de Montfort allowed him time to ride his horse and one day he set off from Widemarsh – a real marsh in those days – and out ran his pursuers until he reached the safety of the Mortimers at Wigmore Castle (See page 35).

During the Wars of the Roses, Hereford supported the Yorkists and the ten main Lancastrian prisoners were executed in Hightown after their capture after the Battle

Left: 14. Hampton Court dining room

Below: 15. Hampton Courtyard

16. Hereford Castle

of Mortimer's Cross (1461). There is still a plaque to commemorate Owen Tudor. During the Great Civil War, the Royalists defended the castle and town but it was captured by Waller's Parliamentarians without difficulty. However, the Parliamentary army didn't stay and Barnabas Scudamore from Holme Lacy, the governor, moved in quickly and the next siege by Lord Leven's Scots army was unsuccessful. The king, with a large force, moved up from Worcester and the Scots vanished. However, this was post-Naseby and he pushed on into Wales leaving the defenders in a sorry state. Colonel Birch and his Parliamentary force (see Goodrich (page 18) moved in and once again Hereford was in Parliamentary hands. After the execution of Charles I the castle was dismantled and the timber and stones sold off, so only the space remains today.

22. HUNTINGTON CASTLE, NR KINGTON

This was a large Norman castle, mostly included in Wales until 1535 when Henry VIII made sure that it was placed on the English side of the border. In King Henry III's time, it belonged to William de Braose, Lord of Brecknock. On his death, his wife held it until 1248 when her daughter married Humphrey de Bohun, son of the Earl of Hereford. Humphrey sided with Simon de Montford in spite of his father fighting for the king. Prince Edward, with help from the two sons of the Earl of Leicester, captured Huntington with Hay and Brecon. De Bohun was captured at Evesham (where Simon was killed) and sent to Beeston Castle, Cheshire, as a prisoner. Here he died but his family continue to hold Huntington and Humphrey, third earl, married the daughter of Edward I, Elizabeth Plantagenet. Humphrey died at the battle of Boroughbridge (1322) where the Barons tried to put down the Despencers, favourites of Edward II.

The castle now passed to the 6th Earl and when he died, his younger daughter married the Earl of Derby who became King Henry IV. The King passed it to the Earl of Buckingham who, in 1403, died fighting for the king at Shrewsbury. His widow, the Countess (the castle had a Countess Tower) asked one Captain Smart, her Constable, to fortify the castle. It was reroofed with shingles and Smart got in a quantity of arrows. The great gate was rehung and today the two bits of stonework that remain on the curtain wall – one a lump of wall and the other a chamber with a stair going up and one down to a dungeon, are all that is left of the Countess's works.

The 2nd Duke (chased by Richard III, took refuge here without luck as he was caught and put to death) had it valued and it was worth nothing at all. In the sixteenth century, one tower was still a prison and there was a Constable but it was all to ruinous to take part in the Civil War.

Ownership passed to Caves, Garnons, Townsends and Holmans and, in 1818, it was the property of Edmund Cheese.

Today it belongs to a local farmer who has cleared the undergrowth. Those wanting to see what is left should park at the village hall and take a short walk into the site where there is still much work to be done.

23. KENTCHURCH

Kentchurch Court, home of the Scudamores, is basically a fourteenth-century fortified mansion. Sir John Scudamore married a daughter of Owain Glyndwr, which was one way of saving his house from attack. There are two motte and baileys in the vicinity, one of which had a Norman chapel that was demolished in the fifteenth century.

Kentchurch Court Gardens are open twice a year under the Yellow Book scheme. For details go to: www.kentchurch.co.uk, (telephone 01981 240228).

24. KILPECK

Kilpeck church with its wonderful carvings both outside and inside is a draw for tourists but few scramble up the motte and bailey to see the castle, which still has two large wall fragments excavated in 1997 (see Shoesmith, 2009, for details). In Domesday, Kilpeck is the property of William Fitz Norman. The castle was in existence by 1124 and William's son Hugh, calling himself 'de Kilpeck', probably rebuilt the castle in stone. He had a chapel in the castle which he gave with the church to St Peter's Monastery in Gloucester. His son, Henry, was fined by King Stephen for trespassing in Haywood Forest, a royal property. Henry died in 1204, leaving a son under age and a widow, Juliana. She gave King John a palfrey and 50 marks so she could now marry whom she chose. Alas, the king chose William Fitzwarren for her as a second husband and William de Cantilupe, her son's ward, looked after the castle. Hugh, when attaining his majority, became custodian of the Royal Forests of Herefordshire. He left two daughters, Isabella who married William de Walerand, a supporter of King Henry III and now the castle owner, and Joan, who married Philip Marmion, hereditary champion of England.

Robert, Isabella's son, left the castle to his nephew, Alan de Plokenet (also spelt Plugenet), a competent soldier, who managed to cultivate a part of Haywood forest – hence the name Alansmore (Allensmore), which we know today as a parish. De Plugenet also obtained an advowson of the grant of Lugwardine and the chapels of Hentland, St Weonards, Llangarron and Little Dewchurch. Alan's son, another Alan, obtained a charter for a weekly market and annual fair at Kilpeck (perhaps the two wrestlers church sculpture and other fair-like images date from this period). The castle then passed to the Earls of Ormonde, devout Lancastrians. The 5th earl was captured at Towton (1467) and beheaded. King Edward IV then granted the castle to Sir William Herbert, Earl of Pembroke, who was captured at Edgecote (1469) and beheaded by the Duke of Clarence. The castle then passed to the 6th earl, who died en route to Jerusalem and after passing to the Boleyn family, one of whom married James St Leger. It passed to the Pyes of the Mynde in Much Dewchurch. Sir William Pye, a Royalist, garrisoned the castle for the king but he became a hostage when Colonel Birch captured Hereford, so the castle was slighted and the owners of the Mynde exchanged it for some other property with the Clive family in 1859.

25. KINGSLAND

A motte and two baileys near the church are all that remain of the De Braose castle, which still had the remains of a keep when visited by Leland in 1530.

26. KINGTON

A clump of trees on a motte at the top of Castle Hill is supposed to be the former home of the Vaughans. It was demolished during King John's reign. The impressive monument to Thomas and Ellen Vaughan (1469) is in the church.

27. KINNERSLEY

The castle of the de la Bere family was really a moated manor house. Remains of the moat can still be seen around the forbidding sixteenth-century 'castle' which was the home of Roger Vaughan, but by the seventeenth century it belonged to the Smallmans whose fine alabaster monument can be seen in the church. In Victorian times the Reavely family lived here and their daughter Minnie married the well-known church architect G. F. Bodley, whose tomb is in the churchyard.

28. LINGEN

Lingen is a small village between Brampton Bryon and Byton. The motte and bailey remains of a shell-keep castle stand near the church. It is believed to be a Mortimer castle which was built by Thurston the Fleming.

29. LLANCILLO

A difficult place to get to, involving a crossing of the Monnow River close to Pontrilas and going under the railway via a farm road to Blancillo Court where there is a field with the church at one end. Before this a motte with remains of a shell-keep of the Esketot family, tenants of the De Lacys of Longtown.

The church is one of the smallest in Herefordshire and belongs to the Friends of Friendless Churches.

30. LONGTOWN CASTLE

Longtown has a small castle in the care of English Heritage Trust, which today consists of a three-storey tower built around 1214 on top of a motte, entered by a wooden stair at the first floor level. The spiral staircase led up to the top where there was a garderobe and a battlement walkway for sentries to keep a lookout.

The bailey was large and went over to the other side of the main road. At one time there would have been gates allowing the road to pass through the castle.

The castle may have been built by William FitzOsbern but soon passed to the De Lacy family. Walter de Lacy was a supporter of King Henry III and his wife, Margaret, founded the Aconbury Nunnery. Walter's younger granddaughter married John de Verdun who died during the Crusades. His son, Theobald, inherited Longtown and his son, the Governor of Ireland, married a Mortimer, Longtown passing to Bartholomew de Burghersh, a supporter of Edward III. His son became a Knight of the Garter and fought at Crecy and Poitiers. Through marriage, Longtown passed to the Despencers – one of them lies in Tewkesbury Abbey – who were invariable on the losing side in the Wars of the Roses. Later, it passed to the Nevilles of Abergavenny.

There is no record of the castle being involved in the Civil War; no doubt it was too ruinous. However, Alfred Watkins writes that the embankment near the keep was the scene of a gibbet where William Jones, who killed his wife by arsenic poisoning in 1790 and was executed at Hereford with his girlfriend, Susannah Rugg, were strung up on the gibbet at Longtown 'to be near to where the deed was committed'.

EHT Open any reasonable daylight hours.

31. LOWER BROCKHAMPTON

Not be confused with Brockhampton-by-Ross with its thatched arts- and crafts-style church, Lower Brockhampton Court is a moated manor with a picturesque gatehouse owned today by the National Trust. The chapel ruins next door are late Norman but the moated manor dates from the fifteenth century and was built by John Domulton with the gatehouse built 1542/43.

NT Open 10.00 a.m. to 4.00 p.m. (5.00 p.m. in summer) Shop and café.

Above: 17. Longtown Bailey and Gate

Left: 18. Longtown Tower

32. LYONSHALL CASTLE

Next to the church, Lyonshall Castle consists today of some of the keep, curtain wall (which was 19 feet high) and extensions to the moat on the north side. Mentioned in Domesday as the property of Walter de Lacy, it was mostly constructed in stone in 1090 by the Devereux family, who were probably related to the Lacy family.

In 1391, Sir John Devereux contracted John Brown, a mason from Hereford, to build a hall and strengthen the gatehouse, and in 1404 the castle was strengthened against Owain Glyndwr but it was in ruins by the end of the fifteenth century.

William Devereux was killed at the Battle of Lewes (1264) fighting for the de Montforts against his king. His land was forfeited but the castle in 1390 was still in Devereux hands as it belonged to Sir John Devereux, Warden of the Cinque Ports and Constable of Dover. Later it passed to an attendant of King Henry V, Sir John Merlaury.

33. MOCCAS

The motte and bailey in Moccas Court Park, no longer visible, was the home of the de Fresne family. The knight's monument in the church is supposed to be de Fresne who Pevsner describes as 'all depressingly crisped-up'. The present owner of Moccas Court uses the park for a runway for his biplane.

34. MONNINGTON COURT

Remains of a motte and ditch stand close to the Court. There is a stone slab in the church believed to be in memory of Owain Glyndwr who is supposed to have spent his last years here in hiding.

35. MUCH MARCLE CASTLE

A large motte and bailey near the church is believed to be the castle of Edmund Mortimer, a supporter of Edward I. His granddaughter Blanche, who married Sir Peter de Grandison and died in 1347, has a beautiful monument in the church. Last year this was repaired and her body, enclosed in a lead coffin, was found and reburied with great dignity. There are other monuments, all in good condition, to the Kyrle family to see in the Kyrle chapel.

36. OLD CASTLETON

The motte and bailey of Old Castleton is two miles downriver of Clifford Castle, which could well be the predecessor of Clifford Castle.

37. PEMBRIDGE CASTLE

Pembridge Castle is situated in Welsh Newton and is an exception to all Hereford castles. It is not a ruin and is a private house now but alas, no longer open on Thursday afternoons. It is 45 metres long and 30 metres wide, with a gatehouse, strong wall, a round keep in the southwest corner and a chapel in the northwest corner. It is surrounded by a dry ditch and dates from the thirteenth century, built by Matilda de Valery but passed to the Pembridge family. Richard de Pembridge was a Knight of the Garter and Warden of the Cinque Ports. It passed to the Burleys, the Tudors and during the Civil War to Sir William Pye, who made it a Royalist outpost. It changed hands in 1644 and was garrisoned by Parliament when ordered for slighting. This was not carried out and George Kemble purchased it after the war and made it habitable. His relation, John Kemble, had an oratory here. It was inhabited by the Scudamores in 1715 and the Townleys, a Jacobite family, before being sold to the Bartletts in 1913, who rebuilt the gatehouse. There are some stone buildings behind and in the chapel a brass to Dr Hedley Bartlett who was a Bishop of Siluria in the lesser Eastern church.

38. PENYARD

A few stones still remain of Penyard Castle up a lane close to Weston-Under-Penyard church. It belonged to the Talbots and is first mentioned in 1338. In the sixteenth century it had a mint and later there was a farmhouse built on the site.

19. Pembridge from the road

20. Pembridge Gatehouse

39. RICHARD'S CASTLE

The name of a small town or a large village near the Welsh border. The motte and bailey close to the old church date from 1086 when it was called Auretone Castle. It belonged to Osborne Fitz Richard. It passed to the Mortimers, Talbots and Popes. The central keep was a shell-keep and the walls around the bailey had four towers – one a solar and one used as a dovecot. In the fifteenth century it was the home of the Vaux family.

Sir William Vaux, a Lanacastrian survivor of Towton, turned up late at the Battle of Tewkesbury (1471) and was killed fighting furiously at the end of the battle; he was buried in Tewkesbury Abbey. His complicated coat-of-arms is well illustrated in *The Street Banners of Tewkesbury*.

During the Civil War the castle belonged to the Salweys, whose monuments are in the church. They were Parliamentary supporters, for Humphry Salwey was a commissioner with the Scots Army who wrote to Governor Scudamore in 1645 advising him to surrender Hereford.

40. SNODHILL

Close to Dorstone, Snodhill is easily seen by a footpath which passes below the scant remains covering 16 acres. The shell-keep was rather thin and the castle must have been most uncomfortable. The Chandos family who owned it later had a much more comfortable farmhouse in Much Marcle, which still survives. In 1436 Richard de la Mare, Sheriff of Hereford, purchased Snodhill from the Bruges family.

Queen Elizabeth passed it to her favourite, Robert Dudley, and in the seventeenth century William Prosser used the stone to rebuild his London house, which had been destroyed, like the castle, during the Civil War when Snodhill was demolished by the Earl of Leven's Scots.

To reach the castle, take the Dorstone-Snodhill lane and at the top of the hill turn left towards Peterchurch. On the right you pass Green House. Next to it there is a gate with five metal hoops and enough space for one person at a time to get through. The ruins are 100 yards further on up a steep slope.

41. STAPLETON CASTLE

Stapleton Castle stands on high ground but the ruins there today are those of an early seventeenth-century house that was built with the stone of an earlier castle. The site has never been properly examined by archaeologists and is very unsafe

Above: 22. Stapleton

Right: 21. Snodhill Ruins

for viewers. A branch of the Stapleton family were Parliamentarians in the Civil War and Sir Philip Stapleton commanded a cavalry detachment at the battle of Edgehill. Severe damage was inflicted on the Royalists but the main parliamentary cavalry was swept away by Prince Rupert's horsemen. The twelfth-century castle belonged to the Lords of Richard's Castle with a large motte with a ditch on both east and west sides. The Cornewall family obtained it at the start of the fifteenth century and up to the Civil War, when Sir Michael Woodhouse advised the Cornewalls to pull down the walls so that it did not become a Parliamentary stronghold – rather like Lingen did with the owners of Wilton Castle at Ross. At the end of the war, the remains of Stapleton were passed to the Harleys at Brampton Bryan. Although the house must have needed extensive repairs, it was inhabited until the nineteenth century as there is a drawing of it in 1850.

For those who like gardens, Mr and Mrs Griffiths open their garden at Stapleton Court four times each year (see Yellow Book published by the National Garden Scheme) and there are guided tours of the ruins at 2.30 p.m. and 3.30 p.m. each day. This is only suitable for good walkers. However, Mrs Griffith's teas are magnificent and worth the £4 admission.

42. STAUNTON-ON-ARROW

A large motte stands close to the church, which has a triangular bailey. Above the village is Waply Hill Fort where Owain Glyndwr and his army camped on one of their forays.

43. TRETIRE

Between Peterstow and Pembridge Castle is the hamlet of Tretire where behind the old vicarage is a rampart with ditch and earthwork remains of Fulk Fitzwarine's thirteenth-century castle. In nearby Michaelchurch is a Roman altar stone cut to form a stoup.
   Fulk Fitzwarine had a motte and bailey castle here. Robinson describes it as a 'large squarish mound on which several towers appear to have stood' and nowadays only a steep bank, a tennis court and a private house mark the site. The church nearby is part of the St Weonards group and has a fourteenth-century coffin lid inside.

44. TREAGO CASTLE

Treago Castle at St Weonards is the home of the Mynors family and is a fortified house built in 1470 by Richard Mynors, a close ally of the Earl of Pembroke, owner of Raglan Castle. It has turrets in each corner – those on the south front being much larger than the other three. The courtyard was filled in in 1844 with

23. Treago

a new staircase and the large tower room has been used as a bedroom, meeting room or card room over the years. The family supported the Yorkists in the War of the Roses and the king in the Civil War. There is a picture of the lady of the house armed only with a dagger keeping out some Scots marauders in 1645. (When cleaned, the picture of Theodosia Mynors shows her clutching a silver-handled black ostrich feather fan and not a silver handled dagger – she still persuaded the Scots to go away.) The house, however, was never attacked so remains little altered over the years. The family has hatchments and monuments in the nearby St Weonards church. There is a large seventeenth-century barn and a walled garden, and for many years the house was used as a farmhouse. The present family had a vineyard and their wine was well valued by local connoisseurs. En route for Treago in 1902, Fletcher Moss had a steep hill to descend when he ran into a herd of swine: 'It was only by the greatest wrench of the bike that I missed one of the milky mothers of the herd only to ride over the fat belly of one of her youngsters promptly turning it into bacon... Then X wanted to know what was the matter with the pigs and thought we ought to go back and pay for any damage. I wanted to know who would have paid me if they had eaten me and my bike.'

Thus, exhausted, they made for Treago, where they are shown around by a general. They show a tiny chamber that had been bricked up until sixty years ago. A skeleton had been found there, believed to have been that of a Roman Catholic priest. They see also shown a painting of Father Harcourt, a Jesuit who had been one of the victims of Titus Oates' conspiracy in the reign of King Charles II. The skeleton may have been one of his friends. Recently the Church of England has been using the castle for meetings.

The castle is open occasionally in the summer months. Apply to Sir Richard Mynors on 01981 580 206.

24. Treago print

25. Urishay

45. URISHAY

Up a steep hill near Peterchurch, Urishay consists today of a ruined manor, a not quite so ruined chapel and a small farm. The manor was lived in until the First World War but was then demolished in the 1920s, and the panelling went to Mull and some to the USA; the owners were the De La Hay family. The castle was originally a motte and bailey with the manor being built on top of the motte. The castle chapel has recently been restored by the Friends of Friendless Churches and the chancel has been repaired, although the nave has been left roofless. The wooden door in the nave can be opened, however, for visitors to see the motte with the castle house on top. The castle is not open to the public.

46. WEOBLEY

In a famous black-and-white village popular with tourists, Weobley castle has some eleventh-century earthwork remains of Walter de Lacy's castle. He was

Sheriff of Hereford and, according to Silas Taylor, who left a seventeenth-century drawing of the castle, it had six round towers and a north gate. Later owners were the Earls of Essex, Dukes of Somerset and the Thynne family. In 1535 it was described by Leland as 'somewhat in decay'.

47. WIGMORE CASTLE

To the end of lane next to the church in Wigmore springs a surprise to any walker. Suddenly, the not inconsequential remains of Wigmore Castle appear, which was the stronghold of the Mortimers. It was built by William FitzOsbern around 1070/71 and is mentioned in Domesday as the possession of Ralph de Mortimer. The Mortimers supported Stephen so when Matilda's son, Henry II, became king, the Mortimers were out of favour. In Henry III's reign, it was Roger Mortimer who had to strengthen his castle as it was the time of the Welsh wars. This Roger welcomed Prince Edward when he escaped from Simon de Montfort, and the Mortimers took part in the Battle of Evesham, which was the downfall of Simon. Another Roger was friendly with Queen Isabella, wife of Edward II, and was one of those involved in the imprisonment and murder of Edward at Berkeley Castle. He was eventually caught by King Edward III and hanged at Tyburn.

The Mortimers continued to flourish and after his capture at Pilleth (1402), Sir Edmund Mortimer married the daughter of Owain Glyndwr. He was rescued by King Henry V and sent to Ireland where he died in 1424. This was almost the end of the castle as it became Crown property but the king preferred Ludlow. In 1601, it became Harley property and was partially dismantled during the Civil War. In 1999, English Heritage Trust reopened the castle but alas, they have not spent any money on it and the ruins are not all that safe. The lack of a suitable car park has meant that few visitors get to it and a much better effort at clearing the ivy and undergrowth would be welcome with sign boards as been done with great success at Montgomery Castle.

EH Open all daylight hours – great care must be taken on some slippery footpaths. (See Appendix I for notes on the Mortimers.)

48. WILTON CASTLE

This castle, recently repaired at some expense by its present owner, opens to the public in the summer months and for an art exhibition in a marquee, usually in the autumn. It was supposed to have been built around 1141 by Hugo de Longchamp. His descendant, Henry de Longchamp, lived there with his daughter, Hawisia, who married William, Lord Fitzhugh. His heiress married into the De Grey family who produced many soldiers and members of parliament. Sir William de Grey was Deputy Governor of Calais who, after a struggle with the Duke of Guise, had to surrender. His ransom was set at the vast sum of 20,000 crowns. Much of the family property had to be sold and the Talbot of Goodrich offered £6000

26. Wigmore

27. Wilton from the
south-east

28. Wilton Castle

for Wilton Castle. The deal was never completed and in Queen Elizabeth's reign the castle was in the hands of Sir John Brydges, Deputy Governor of the Tower of London. It was his delay that saved the life of the young Princess Elizabeth when she was imprisoned in the tower.

During the Civil War, Sir John Brydges decided that he was neither a Royalist nor a Parliamentarian and went off to Ireland. When he returned, the Royalists Henry Lingen and Lord Scudamore were so annoyed with Brydges for not allowing a garrison in his castle house that, waiting until he was in church, they sent their men to burn it down. In the nineteenth century, a small house was constructed in the south-eastern corner, where the present owners live. The title of Lord Grey of Wilton was revived in 1784 and the family became merged with the Grosvenors. So those who think Cromwell knocked down the castles in Herefordshire must think again. It seems that it was nothing but spite, because as a seventeenth-century castle, Wilton would never have stood up to a siege.

Open early June under Yellow Book Garden scheme. Contact Mr and Mrs Parslow. EHT members free www.wiltoncastle.co.uk

Above: 30. Wilton East Tower

Right: 31. Wilton Elizabethan house

SHROPSHIRE CASTLES

49. ACTON BURNELL

In 1284 Bishop Burnell, having entertained King Edward I here, obtained a licence to crenellate his house. There are remains of a moat, but it is surprising he did not turn his house into a real castle.

In 1293, the king held a parliament in the great barn here. Among other things discussed were the rights of small business folk to get their outstanding bills paid by a certain time – a subject that perhaps needs to be discussed by Parliament today.

The castle consists of a rectangular building, 95 feet by 60 feet, with a square tower in each corner. The bishop's daughter married Lord Lovell. The castle then passed to the Duke of Norfolk and lastly to Robert Dudley.

EHT Open any reasonable time in daylight hours. Car park. No shop or café.

50. ALBERBURY

On the B4393 a few miles west of Shrewsbury, the remains of Alberbury Castle can be seen close to the church. It is constructed in local red sandstone and it has not weathered well. The owner was Fulk de Fitzwarin in King John's reign when the castle acted as a barrier to stop the Welsh attacking Shrewsbury. The castle bailey wall was repaired during the Civil War when it was briefly reoccupied. The church next door has a large tower which could have been used as a lookout.

51. ALBRIGHT HUSSEY

Close to Shrewsbury Battlefield, Albright Hussey is half timbered and half stone and was built in 1601. It has a moat and one of the Hussey women married a Corbet. During the Civil War it was garrisoned by the Royalists in 1642. The

Above: 32. Acton Burnell

Right: 33. Alberbury

Parliamentary attack on a Sunday afternoon was thwarted by Sergeant Preece who shot one of the attackers. Today, it is a small restaurant.

52. APLEY CASTLE

Alan de Charlton obtained a licence to crenellate his house in 1327. The house in the picture was demolished and its predecessor because in the 1600s Francis Charlton's widow married Thomas Hanmer, who spent £6,000 on a new house which he fortified for King Charles I in the Civil War. It was captured and dismantled, the lead being used to repair Shrewsbury Castle.

When Bromfield's new house was built for Sir John Charlton in 1791, the old castle was turned into stables but little remains of it today. The Bromfield house has also been demolished to make way for Telford's new buildings.

34. Apley

53. BISHOP'S CASTLE

The Bishop of Hereford had a castle here built at the end of the eleventh century. It was unpopular with the bishops due to its remoteness and nearness to the Welsh border. During the Baron's War, the bishop was captured by Simon de Montfort and sent to Eardisland. The Constable was killed and John Fitz Alan stole thirty-two horse loads of wheat, six crossbows and six halberts, one without a head. Leland says the castle was still habitable in 1530 but today it consists of a few walls by the Castle Hotel and the bowling green. Below the green there is a small public park and some more walls.

54. BRIDGNORTH

Robert de Bellèsme built Bridgnorth Castle on a sandy promontory close to the present day railcar station. The town was fortified by the Saxons but in 1102 it was captured by Henry I and given to Hugh de Mortimer. The latter supported Stephen and was unable to stop the king capturing Bridgnorth in 1155. The town was fortified again with King John providing an outer bailey and barbican (demolished finally when the post office was built in 1901). The Royalists were here during the Civil War when the defences were still viable. However, the Parliamentary army used men to tunnel under the walls so in 1646 Sir Robert Howard was forced to surrender. The rectangular keep was blown up and, having been undermined, fell at a strange angle so only this and the North Gate remains today. On the other side of the Severn Valley railway is Panpudding Hill where there are remains of a ringwork and platform used by the Parliamentary artillery during the siege.

Castle Park is open at all daylight hours and has seats for visitors.

Above: 35. Bishop's Castle

Right: 36. Bridgnorth

55. BROCKHURST

There is a large motte and two baileys in a wooded area south of Church Stretton. The castle was erected by Henry II to keep the Mortimers at bay. It was reinforced by Richard I and by the Nevilles, who were ejected by the Fitz Alans. After passing to Hubert de Burgh and Henry de Hastings, it was abandoned in 1255 but much remains.

56. BRONCROFT

Close to Diddlebury is the castellated house, Broncroft Castle, built by Seddon in 1868 but incorporating the castle that Roger Tyrell had in the fourteenth century. It passed to the Burleys and Sir Simon Burley was an advisor to Richard II but his many enemies succeeded in getting him executed in 1386. Passing through many owners, it was held by Parliamentary troops in the Civil War. The Royalists attacked the garrison but they could not prevent the partial demolition of the castle after the war. The Lutleys repaired it and nowadays it is difficult to see which pieces belong to the original building.

57. BURFORD (NR TENBURY)

A moated manor house belonging to the Cornewall family was replaced in 1728 by Burford House. In the church is the grave of Elizabeth Cornewall (1326) who was the daughter of John of Gaunt and wife of Sir John Cornewall who lived in

37. Broncroft

the castle. There are many other Cornewall tombs to be seen including a brass to another Elizabeth who died in 1354.

58. CASTLE PULVERBATCH

A large motte and bailey remain of Roger Venator's castle. It passed to the Kilpecks and later to Ralph Boteler.

59. CAUS CASTLE

Near Westbury only earthworks remain of the Corbet's motte and bailey castle built on the site of an iron-age hill fort. In 1630 it belonged to the Thynnes, having been a prison by the Staffords in the fifteenth century. During the Civil War it surrendered to the Parliamentarians and was demolished. Fletcher Moss and X came here on their cycles in 1902. 'A puncture and refreshment delay us, then ... we come again nearly to the Bottom of Caus Hill, nearly to where we were (before).' 'X' takes a photo of Fletcher in his splendid cycle outfit complete with spats.

60. CHARLTON

Not far from Wellington at Wrockwardine, John de Charlton obtained a licence to crenellate his house in 1317. The moat still remains but little else does.

38. Caus and F. Moss

61. CHENEY LONGVILLE

Robert Cheney obtained a licence to crenellate his house 2 miles north-west of Craven Arms. Castle farm still has a large courtyard with a guardroom next to the gatehouse, now just an ordinary entrance. The castle farm was built in the nineteenth century and the ownership passed to the Plowdens then the Beddoes families. Some cannonballs remain from a bombardment by Parliamentary guns in the Civil War.

62. CLUN

One of Shropshire's larger castles, Clun Castle keep still stands proudly on a vast motte surrounded on three sides by the River Clun. In the eleventh century it belonged to Picot de Say and passed by marriage to the Fitz Alans, who held it until it was a ruin in the 1540s when it passed to the Duke of Norfolk. Salter says the keep building is in fact the solar, similar to that at Grosmont with the fireplace and the Lord's chamber above.

The north bailey is now a bowling green and there is a causeway to the other bailey. The foundations of two semi-circular towers on the motte still remain.

EHT Open at any reasonable daylight hours.

39. Clun Castle print

40. Clun – modern ruin

63. CORFHAM

Near Diddlesbury, Corfham Castle belonged to the Cliffords then passing to John Giffard. When he died in 1299, it was very ruinous. Today just a few mounds in a field remain.

64. ELLESMERE

A large flat motte and bailey occupy the top of the hill here. They mark the site of a castle built by Roger de Montgomery in the late eleventh century. It was given to Llywelyn by King John as a dowry for his daughter Joan but taken back when the Welsh invaded. Henry III repaired it and later it passed to the Strange family. Young Lord Strange was held as a hostage by King Richard III at the Battle of Bosworth and was lucky to escape with his life.

42. High Ercall

65. HIGH ERCALL

A few miles northeast of Shrewsbury, High Ercall Hall was built by Lord Newport in 1608 and fortified for the Royalists in the Civil War. Sir William Vaughan led a Royalist successful defence of the house when attacked by Parliamentarians. Lord Newport was heavily fined and driven abroad after the Civil War. The modern house has few remains of his home.

66. HOLDGATE CASTLE

South of Shipton in the Corve Valley, Holdgate Castle is now a farmhouse built inside the bailey. Known as 'Helgot's Castle' at the time of Domesday, it became a property of Bishop Burnell in 1284. There is still a large drum tower incorporated into the building. At one time it belonged to Lord Lovell.

67. HOPTON CASTLE

The square keep of this castle remains on a motte, which had two baileys and a deep moat. 5 miles southeast of Clun, the twelfth-century castle of Osbert de Hopton was strengthened by the addition of the stone keep in the fourteenth century. It was briefly possessed by the Corbets who sold it to the Wallops, and in 1643 they put in a Parliamentary garrison under Samuel More. Revd Webb in his *Memorials of the Civil War* describes what happened next: 'Every mother's son was stripped, tied back to back, and put to death with circumstances of the utmost barbarity.' More was kept by Woodhouse, the Royalist commander, as a prisoner.

The castle was comprehensively repaired in 2010 and 2011. It was reopened by the Duke of Gloucester in December 2011. It is more of a home than a castle.

Friends of Hopton Castle. Open at all times. Small car park. Leaflet guide.

43. Castle/Holdgate

44. Hopton Castle tower and moat

68. KNOCKIN

Between Shrewbury and Oswestry a motte in a wood close to the church is all that remains of Lord Strange's castle. Their badge was a greyhound. It later belonged to the Stanleys.

69. LANGLEY HALL

Home of the Lees, who were Royalists during the Civil War and heavily were fined. It had a crenellated wall. It was demolished in Victorian times, but the gatehouse has since been repaired by the Landmark Trust who let it for six people. The chapel nearby is in the care of English Heritage Trust and has a service every September.

EHT Chapel open at all reasonable daylight hours

70. LUDLOW CASTLE

The most important of all of the castles in this book, Ludlow was the centre of the government of the Marches. Originally built by Walter de Lacy, second in command to William FitzOsbern of Chepstow and Earl of Hereford – his son Roger completed it. Sited on a high plateau and surrounded on three sides by the River Teme, it is only on the town side that it was vulnerable. In the twelfth century a large outer bailey was built with two small towers and surprisingly not much of an outer gateway.

In 1425, Richard, Duke of York, inherited the castle so that when his son, victor of the Battle of Mortimer's Cross in 1461, became King Edward IV, the castle belonged to the king; the Princes in the Tower, Edward and Richard, were brought up here. Young Edward was also to be Edward V on the death of his father in 1483 but Richard III seized the throne and the young princes were murdered mysteriously in the Tower of London.

The Tudors lived here in style and in 1493 Henry VII gave the castle to his highly popular son, Prince Arthur. He only lived another nine years, alas, so the scene was set for Henry VIII. However, the Prince's Council became established here at Ludlow as a Marcher government.

45. Hopton Tower

46. Ludlow from the air

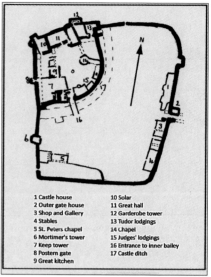

1 Castle house   10 Solar
2 Outer gate house   11 Great hall
3 Shop and Gallery   12 Garderobe tower
4 Stables   13 Tudor lodgings
5 St. Peters chapel   14 Chapel
6 Mortimer's tower   15 Judges' lodgings
7 Keep tower   16 Entrance to inner bailey
8 Postern gate   17 Castle ditch
9 Great kitchen

Above: 48. Ludlow Gatehouse

Right: 47. Ludlow plan

Many literary characters have connections with Ludlow Castle. Henry Sidney, Lord President of the Council, was the son of Sir Philip Sidney, the poet. The Earl of Bridgewater was president in 1643 when Milton performed his *Comus* masque in the castle grounds. This heralded a tradition of open air-theatre that went on for years.

Alas, in William and Mary's reign, the Marcher government was dissolved and the castle started to decay. It was abolished in 1689 but not before a new regiment was formed here and marched off to the Irish ferry in Cheshire to take part fighting for William at the Battle of the Boyne.

In 1811, the castle was purchased by Edward Clive, Earl of Powis, son of Robert Clive of India. It has remained their property ever since.

Fletcher Moss, after arguing with the custodian over the shilling entrance in 1902, took some photographs, especially of the round chapel. The panelling of the chapel is now in the Bull Inn which 'would have been an excuse for wanting cider'. They shot down 'that terrible hill, through the narrow gate and across the Teme'. They then went on to Richards' Castle.

LORDS PRESIDENT OF THE COUNCIL OF WALES

It was not until the reign of Henry VIII that in 1536 the president of the council, Sir Rowland Lee, and his advisors decided that Wales was no longer an enemy and the Marches became counties, so boroughs and counties a few years later were bestowed on Wales. Military power gave way to civil power and, according to Wright, 'tumults subsided, obedience was restored, peace, order and civilisation followed in the train of liberty'.

Ludlow still controlled the Southern Marches, but the Northern Marches were controlled from Chester and later Rhuddlan castles. There was also a council based

50. Ludlow Chapel

51. Ludlow from west

in York for the Northern counties. The previous president, John Voysey, was tutor to Princess (later Queen) Mary as well as Bishop of Exeter. In 1534 Sir Rowland Lee, Bishop of Lichfield, was Lord President of 'The Court for the Government of Wales' as it was then known. Lee was buried at St Chad's Shrewsbury and the Shrewsbury chronicle said 'he would make the white sheep keep the black' and he 'brought Wales, being at his coming very wild, into good civility before he died'.

From 1543 to 1548, Richard Sampson, also Bishop of Lichfield was president. He was replaced by John Dudley, Earl of Warwick and Duke of Northumberland, but as a supporter of Lady Jane Grey he did not last long. In 1549, Sir William Herbert, Earl of Pembroke, was president and persuaded King Henry to marry his sixth wife, Pembroke's sister, Catherine Parr. Pembroke was a soldier and on Elizabeth's accession he was responsible for putting down Wyatt's rebellion and became Captain-Geneneral of her army overseas. In 1553, Nicholas Heath, Bishop of Worcester, was president then, in 1555, Gilbert Bourne, Bishop of Bath and Wells. After him, Queen Mary made Lord Williams of Thame her Lord Chamberlain and President. He died in the first year of Queen Elizabeth's reign (1558) and was succeeded as president by Sir Henry Sidney, father of poet and soldier Sir Philip Sidney. The next appointment was Henry Sidney's son-in-law, Henry Earl of Pembroke. He died in 1601 and was succeeded by Lord Zouche of Codnore (died 1605).

In Ludlow church is the tomb of Ralph, Lord Eure, President from 1610 to 1612. The next president, Lord Gerald of Bromley, entertained Prince Charles (later King Charles I) at Ludlow with much pomp and ceremony. In 1617, it was William, Earl of Northampton as Lord President.

William died in 1630 and was succeeded by Sir John Egerton, Earl of Bridgewater. King Charles I visited Ludlow again 'amidst the discharge of great guns and firelocks of the soldiers, attended by all the officers magnificently dressed and mounted; and so great was the pomp, that the like thereof was never before seen in these parts'. During the Civil War, Bridgewater's council was not able to carry out its duties and seems to have been ineffective during Cromwell's protectorate. Judge Littleton, a Welsh judge, was a leading member of Charles II's Council of the Marches and in 1667, the Marquis and Earl of Worcester was Lord President, and from 1679–92 it was Prince Rupert's turn. In 1684, Sir John Bridgeman was Lord President. He was a strict person, always shutting people up in the porter's lodge. One of those he shut up said when he died, 'Here lies Sir John Bridgeman, clad in his clay, God said to the Devil, Sirrah take him away.'

His tomb is in St Laurence's church, Ludlow. Finally, the last Lord President was Viscount Brandon. The post then ceased after the 1688 revolution. Lord Herbert of Cherbury took the castle in December in the name of the Prince of Orange and the Catholic sheriff of Worcester and Sir Walter Blount were imprisoned therein.

Powis Castle Estates. Shop, café in outer gatehouse. Telephone 01584 873355 for times of opening *(www.ludlowcastle.com)*.

71. MORE

A well-preserved motte and bailey supposed to have been William de Botterell's castle as he obtained a licence to fortify it in 1195.

72. MORETON CORBET

A rather disappointing castle but a church full of Corbet tombs. Moreton Corbet, once known as Moreton Toret as it belonged to the Toret family, was obtained by the Corbets by marriage in 1230. The Elizabethan house that stands in ruins there today was started in 1560 by Sir Andrew Corbet and some say was never really completed. Sir Andrew was Vice-President of the Council of the Marches so wanted somewhere smarter than an old ruin to live in. Unfortunately, during the Civil War the castle was attacked by a small group of Parliamentarians who captured it at night. The family returned after the war and repaired part of the house but they later moved to a more comfortable home at Preston Brockhurst.

EHT Open daylight hours. Small car park.

73. MYDDLE

In 1902 a lonely tower still stood of Myddle Castle. There is now only a bit of stair turret. This was Lord Strange's house in 1308 when he obtained a licence to crenellate it. In 1700 it still had a gatehouse and a building around a square courtyard. Richard Gough, author of *Antiquities and Memoirs of the Parish of Myddle* relates how as a schoolboy he witnessed a Civil War skirmish when a Royalist Irish Cornet argued with a woman over a bed he was going to take, said it was 'too coarse' and threw it in the lake. A nearby patrol of Parliamentary soldiers shot him and he was placed on the self-same bed where he was taken by his Royalist friends to Shrawardine the next day; here he died. Fletcher Moss describes the castle as 'ruined, surrounded by a moat and the little island all grown over with potatoes'. He took his photograph and then left with 'X' up a steep hill.

74. OSWESTRY

Built at Domesday by Reginald de Balliol, Oswestry Castle passed to the Fitz Alans of Clun. It withstood being sacked by the Parliamentarians. Today the motte remains in a park. Bailey Head Square is where the bailey was sited. In the sixteenth century it belonged to Thomas Howard who lost his life after supporting Mary Queen of Scots.

Above: 52. Morton Corbet

Right: 53. Myddle Castle

75. QUATFORD

Close to Bridgnorth, Roger de Montgomery built a motte and bailey castle here, but abandoned it when the opportunity came to move into Bridgnorth and his son, Robert de Bellème moved there in 1101 to start Bridgnorth Castle. Quatford also has a modern (1829) castle on a crag with battlements built by a local architect.

76. RED CASTLE

The Audleys had a castle here, obtaining a licence from King Henry III in 1228. The remains are in Hawkstone Park on two ridges, with a couple of tall towers of red sandstone and an unfinished, very long ditch joining the two ridges.

  The hill is not open to the public. Strangely, there are several retired Shropshire policemen who wear the Red Castle tie with the number 17 on it. This was because the village of Weston-under-Red Castle was the scene in 1968 of a siege. A farmer, armed with a shotgun, kept his wife and four children locked up for seventeen days before falling asleep so that his wife was able to throw the gun out of the window to the police. The farmer was sent to Broadmoor.

77. ROWTON

At Alberbury, Rowton Castle is a nineteenth-century building built on the site of a medieval castle that belonged to the de Says. It was destroyed by a Welsh raid and rebuilt it in grand style by the Lysters to the design of George Wyatt in 1809–12.

78. RYTON

Three lumps of masonry in the churchyard of Ryton-XI-Towns are all that can be seen of Edmund, Earl of Arundel's castle, once property of the Stranges. The keep ruin had a cottage built into it at that has vanished. Ryton Towers, on the road to Knockin is a Victorian mansion built for the Walfords.

  The castle seems to have consisted of only one tower and inside the church there is a well-constructed continuous DVD showing the work needed to restore the ruins, a picture of the thatched cottage built into them and much of interest.

79. SHRAWARDINE

West of Shrewsbury, close to Montfort is the motte and some pieces of masonry belonging to Shrawardine Castle. It was the property of Rainald de Ballieul at the time of Domesday, then destroyed by the Welsh in 1215. Henry III gave it to Joan Fitz Alan with order to repair it. In the fifteenth century it passed to the Bromleys, one of whom presided over the trial of Mary Queen of Scots. During the Civil War,

54. Ruyton Tower ruins

55. Shrawardine
towards the River
Severn

56. Shrawardine ruins

it was strongly garrisoned by Colonel Vaughan for the king. On one occasion, he led a sally but on returning to his castle was captured by Colonel Mytton, and a small force of Parliamentarians. The castle defenders, seeing their leader captured, prepared to lift the drawbridge and Vaughan jumped onto it as it was going up and escaped. In 1645, the castle finally surrendered and was demolished, the stones going into repairs to the walls of Shrewsbury.

80. SHREWSBURY CASTLE

The castle at Shrewsbury was built by Robert de Montgomery with a high earth motte at a narrow neck of the River Severn so that there was a mere 300 yards to defend. It passed into the King's hands and Edward I used it as a base for armed sallies into Wales. Town walls were built in 1220 to 1242 after attacks by Llywelyn the Great. There is a stretch of wall still surviving, best seen from the river. The gate is about all that is left of Norman times, but there is a barbican dating from Civil War times. The motte now has Laura's Tower on top, built as is the hall block by Thomas Telford, c.1790.

The hall now contains the excellent Shropshire Regimental Museum. For opening times, telephone 01743 262292.

81. STAPLETON

Not to be confused with Stapleton near Presteigne, Stapleton is off the A49 close to Shrewsbury. There is a farm there called Moat Farm, where the plinths of a fortified house remain.

It was the home of the branch of the Stapleton family who were sheriffs of Shropshire in the fourteenth and fifteenth centuries. It had a gatehouse that was demolished in the 1930s.

82. STOKESAY CASTLE

Best seen from the Hereford–Shrewsbury train, this is one of the gems of the Welsh Marches. It was constructed as a fortified mansion by Lawrence of Ludlow, a wealthy wool merchant who obtained a licence to crenellate in 1291. It is one of the few buildings of that date that hasn't been spoiled; the new gatehouse built by the Earl of Craven just before the Civil War and the lowering of the courtyard walls after that war are the only changes.

It was acquired by the Allcrofts in Victorian times and they put in some much needed repairs without spoiling anything. English Heritage Trust took over in 1992. There is no chapel; the family used the nearby church. The medieval hall with its high roof has a hearth in the middle but no chimney. One wonders how often it was used?

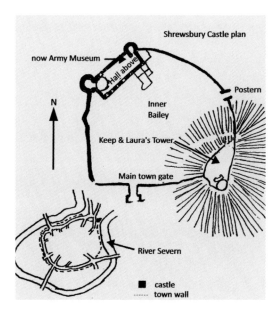

Left: 57. Shrewsbury plan

Right: 58. Shrewsbury Castle Gate

The living quarters on top of the south tower are jettied out on stone corbels. Two storeys lead to the top, no longer possessing a plastered ceiling. The fireplace hood is also missing but very little else. There is a private garderobe and with the fire working it must have been quite comfortable.

The north tower has rooms at three levels, all empty today but probably used for guests. The open roof is a Victorian Allcroft construction.

Lawrence was drowned at sea off Suffolk in 1294 and eventually the castle passed by marriage to the Vernons. Spendthrift Henry Vernon ended up in Fleet Prison. He sold Stokesay to Sir George Mainwaring, but he ran out of money and sold it on to a rich widow, Dame Elizabeth Craven, in 1620 for £13,500 – a considerable sum of money then. Her son, young William, became a soldier but instead of strengthening Stokesay during the Civil War, he surrendered it meekly to a Parliamentary force. Fortunately it was not slighted and the Royalist attempt to recapture it the following year resulted in the destruction of the church and the death of Lord Croft. (See Croft Castle page 17).

EHT Open April to September, daily 10.00 a.m. to 6.00 p.m. October to 2 November 10.00 a.m. to 5.00 p.m., 2 November to 15 February: Saturday and Sunday 10.00 a.m. to 4.00 p.m., 16 February to 20 February, daily 10.00 a.m. to 4.00 p.m. Closed 24 December to 1 January. Tearoom open 1 April to 2 November. No dogs in castle. Car parking.
Telephone 01588 672544 for further information. Family tickets and concession for OAPs available.

Counterclockwise from top: 62. Stokesay from across the lake

60. Stokesay North Tower

61. Stokesay postcard

59. Stokesay plan

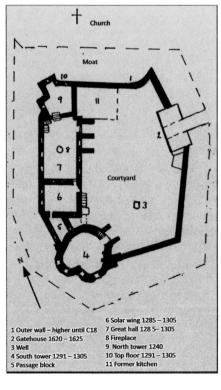

1 Outer wall – higher until C18	6 Solar wing 1285 – 1305
2 Gatehouse 1620 – 1625	7 Great hall 128 5– 1305
3 Well	8 Fireplace
4 South tower 1291 – 1305	9 North tower 1240
5 Passage block	10 Top floor 1291 – 1305
	11 Former kitchen

83. TONG

Tong castle was the property of the Zouche family. It was then described as crenellated by Fulk de Pembridge who obtained a licence from Richard II in 1381. The Vernons of Haddon Hall held it during the Civil War and it was not demolished although a Royalist stronghold. It was Capability Brown who built the new mansion (pulled down in 1954) and the M54 motorway that finally destroyed this building. There are Vernons buried in Tong church, which is well worth a visit.

The church still shows scars of war where it was attacked by Parliamentary cannon during the Civil War. A stone cannon ball, found many years ago, is sitting on a shelf in the vestry next to the candles and candlesticks. In the porch is a stone carving of the castle with three towers, the centre an elaborate affair. There is a monument to George Durant, last owner of the old castle who made his money as clerk to the army paymaster in the West Indies in the eighteenth century. He died young in 1780 and his memorial reads:

> His sentiments were liberal
> His disposition humane
> His manners polished
> Happy alike in his mental
> And in his personal accomplishments.

84. UPTON CRESSET

Home of the Cash family – William Cash MP has moved out and his son is now there in his place – Upton Cresset is an Elizabethan house with a fine twin-towered gatehouse. There is also a dry moat. The Cressets were sheriffs of Shropshire. Edward Cresset was a member of Charles I's council and one of the planners to extricate him from Carisbrooke Castle in the Isle of Wight. Another Cresset played a part in the negotiations between court and government during the madness of King George III. The little church next door is now in the hands of the Churches Conservation Trust.

Open May – October, Thursdays 2.30 p.m. – 5.00 p.m. Parties by appointment. Telephone 01746 714308 or go to www.uptoncresset.co.uk for further details. The gatehouse is let out as a flat.

85. WATTLESBOROUGH

In Alberbury, Wattlesborough Hall today is a large farmhouse incorporating a square tower, believed to have been built by the Corbets in the thirteenth century, which was heightened in the fifteenth century. Acton states that there were three towers and there are steps going up to the roof, which was originally battlemented. It passed to the Mouthés, the Burghs and the Leightons. They moved and the farmhouse was added to the tower in the eighteenth century.

63. Tong Church

64. Tong Church
cannonball

65. Upton Cresset
print

Above: 67. Wattlesborough

Right: 66. Upton Cresset gatehouse

86. WEM

Remains of a motte near the church are all to show of the Pantuff family castle, which was built during King John's reign. It passed to the Butlers and was repaired in 1314 by Hugh Fitz Aer who was a tenant of William Butler. The Fitz Aers had to supply one man with a lance to keep the castle fire going if the other members of the garrison were outside. During the Civil War Wem was held by Parliamentary forces, and a Royalist force under Lord Capel failed to capture it.

87. WHITCHURCH

William de Warenne owned a castle here in 1240, known as Pan Castle, just southwest of the town, and some remains of the motte and bailey are still visible. It was taken over by the Le Strange family but Fulk Le Strange moved to Blakemere, east of the town, where he obtained a licence to crenellate his manor in 1332 from Edward II. Blakemere was ruined during the Civil War and in the eighteenth century stone from the ruin was used to repair the parish church.

88. WHITTINGTON

This is a complex castle close to Oswestry. Originally belonging to the Peverels, it passed to the de Veres and later to Roger de Powys. It was Fulk Warin, though, who obtained a licence to fortify it against the Welsh, by Henry III in 1221.

68. Whittington entrance

Numerous Fulks held it for years until 1415 when it passed by marriage to the Bouchiers. Sir William Bouchier was executed by Henry VI and it later passed to the Earl of Arundel. Although complete in 1545, it fell into decay. The Lloyds of Aston repaired the outer gatehouse which was lived in until 2001, and created a trust so that the castle is open to the public.

There were two medieval courts at Whittington: a Court Leet dealing with minor affairs and and Court Baron with more important affairs. The National Library of Wales has many records of these courts.

Ivo FitzWarin, who was in charge of the castle during the Glyndwr Rising, had trouble with raiders, mostly stealing food and animals. Thus he was discharged from paying rent while he helped his tenants to survive. His brass can be seen in Wantage Church, Berkshire, in full armour but only 5 feet in height.

The castle consists of an inner gatehouse with curtain wall and remains of five circular towers. The old keep remains are inside the inner bailey. There is a wall of the fourteenth-century hall remaining where the family lived and it is likely the keep was demolished in King John's time and never fully repaired. Bits of the towers have been used to repair the Halston road, but what remains is one of Shropshire's most unusual castles as it was defended by water. The outer bailey is now used as the car park but once had a beautiful garden.

Whittington Castle Preservation Trust. Open all reasonable daylight hours. Shop, café and car park.

Left: 69. Whittington Round Keep

Right: 70. Whittington Keep

71. Whittington water defences

WELSH BORDERS

89. BRECON

Beside the Usk and Honddu river junction, Brecon Castle was founded by Bernard of Newmarch around 1093. The bailey is now occupied by a hotel and the motte in the bishop's house gardens. Ely tower and the shell keep were possibly built by the De Braose family and the hall area by Humphrey de Bohun in the thirteenth century. Not much survives.

90. CHEPSTOW

William the Conqueror's right-hand man, William FitzOsbern was the first builder of mighty Chepstow Castle. He was made Earl of Hereford and, to tackle the Welsh, he followed up Chepstow with castles at Monmouth, Hereford, Ewyas Harold, Clifford and Wigmore. On William's death his son Roger de Breteuil took over, but as he had been involved in a plot against his King, Chepstow passed to the King and, in 1115, it passed to the de Clares. Gilbert de Clare took over Chepstow and on his death the castle passed to his wealthy daughter Isabella, a minor but a ward of King Henry II.

Enter the Marshals. William Marshal was known as the Champion of England. His effigy can be seen in Temple church, London – a tall, long-legged knight in chainmail, clutching a long Norman shield and a broken sword. His belt strap is far too long as if he had been on a diet for some time. William served four kings and married Isabella, so the modifications to Chepstow Castle mostly belong to him and his sons. The Marshals built an east bailey, the twin drum-towered main gatehouse with a western barbican, with another tower to protect its southwest corner. All this was on a narrow ridge overlooking the Wye. The guidebook shows an ingenious rope lift that worked from a vault down to the river and could lift stores or even a person from a boat below.

When Anselm, the last son, died in 1245, Chepstow had become a considerable fortress. The next owner, Roger Bigod, grandson of Maud Marshal, Anselm's sister,

72. Brecon

73. Chepstow
from the river

was Earl of Norfolk. He built the chapel, improved the living accommodation, enlarging the south-east bailey tower to make further accommodation and added kitchen, buttery and further rooms against the bailey wall.

Roger was also responsible for the town gate, later used as a prison and a wall going from barbican to river. He also provided money for Tintern Abbey. When he died – in debt – the castle passed to the Crown but was used by King Edward II's favourites from time to time. The Norfolks garrisoned it against Owain Glyndwr and the Woodvilles, Yorkist relations of the queen, were taken out by Warwick the 'King Maker' after the Lancastrian victory of Edgecote (1469) and executed at Kenilworth.

In Tudor times, Chepstow was held by a cousin of Henry VII, Charles, Earl of Worcester. He had a great deal of ability, even on the theatrical side. As Lord Chamberlain to Henry VIII, he was responsible for the amazing Field of the Cloth of Gold, when Henry and Francis I of France met near Calais with lots of pageantry, a mock palace, ornate tents etc. For his many services, the Earl and his wife were buried in an elaborate tomb in the Royal Chapel, Windsor.

Left: 75. Chepstow main hall

Right: 76. Chepstow Merton Tower

During the Civil War, Chepstow was held by the Herberts of Raglan for King Charles I. The hundred-strong garrison held out for only three days after a breach was made by Sir Thomas Morgan's Parliamentary cannon. In the second Civil War, Sir Nicholas Kemeys seized the castle but Colonel Bride's men forced another breach and the garrison surrendered. Kemeys was shot on the spot.

At the Restoration, Henry Marten, a leading regicide, was imprisoned in Marten's tower for twenty years. When he died, he was buried in the chancel of Chepstow church. However, in the eighteenth century the vicar of Chepstow, Thomas Chest, a devout Royalist, removed Marten's coffin to some other place. Hence the epitaph:

> Here lies at rest, it is confest
> One Chest within another.
> The chest of wood was very good
> But who say so of t'other.

The last private owner of Chepstow was a Mr Lysaght, who in 1953 put the castle in the care of the Ministry, now CADW.

The Lysaghts came from Ireland and were joint owners of the Chepstow Racecourse as well as a steelworks in Wales. When I first came to live in the south of Herefordshire, Ross bookshop was run by relations of theirs, Mr and

74. Chepstow Kemeys Memorial

Mrs D Lysaght. I attended the funeral of Dermot Lysaght along with a general and an admiral who were happy to talk to an ex-RAF national servicemen who never reached a higher rank than senior aircraftsman.

CADW. Open at daylight hours. If ticket office closed, try shop. Car park (£1 an hour), tourist office and museum nearby. The white bridge is a popular spot for taking photographs of the castle. It is two minutes walk from the car park.

91. HAY-ON-WYE

The first castle at Hay was a motte and bailey close to the church, called the 'Tumpy' by locals, which was built *c.* 1100 by Revell, a knight of Henry I's reign. The present castle was built by the De Broase family 100 years later. William de Braose's wife Maud was a ferocious woman nicknamed 'Mol Walbee'. She upset King John who set fire to the castle and put Maud in Corfe Castle dungeon where she died of starvation. The de Braose family hung onto the castle, which was burnt again in 1231 by Prince Lewellyn. Eva de Braose refortified the town and the castle eventually passed to the Dukes of Buckingham. In 1521, when the third duke was beheaded, the castle lost its importance and became a ruin. The Jacobean house next to it was built by the Gwynns. In 1937, it was purchased by Ben Guinness MP but two years later the roof caught fire and the fine staircase was burnt down and much of the fine plaster-work destroyed. In the 1960s it and the castle were purchased by Richard Booth, 'the uncrowned King of Hay', who set up Hay as the second-hand book centre of Wales and more recently helped establish the

77. Hay Castle and House

78. Hay Castle Tower

famous Hay Festival. The Jacobean addition is supported by ivy and its timbers are suffering from death-watch beetle, so plans for its restoration are in hand.

Some parts of the castle are open to the public. (Telephone 01497 820503, email: books@haycastle.demon.co.uk)

92. MONTGOMERY

High above the small town of Montgomery, the remains of Montgomery Castle look out over the countryside. It is then a surprise that this castle was not built until 1223 during the minority of King Henry III. Plans must have been made before as palisades were made by carpenters in Much Wenlock and twenty Forest of Dean miners arrived to cut out the ditches and the huge wall. Montgomery is one of the first castles to have two gatehouses but the south side was open to

Montgomery. Castle Keep

79. Montgomery

attack. In 1282 the castle had a prison as a document exists showing the charges made by the governor to the king:

> Holy Vaughan and his son David with their two Welsh pages, 106 days at *6d* a day and for a further 128 days for David alone at *2d* a day.

There was an error in the addition so that the document was queried and David was charged more. Fletcher Moss, who mentions this, says 'perhaps he [David] had a big appetite'.

During the Civil War the Herberts surrendered the castle to Colonel Myddleton. The castle and the Herbert's wooden buildings were all destroyed. When excavated in the 1960s, the ditch was found to contain masses of Civil War armour.

CADW. Open at all times. No guidebook, shop or cafe. There are a few interesting information boards and a small car park.

93. MONMOUTH

Two ruined rooms which interlock at an angle are all that remain of Monmouth Castle, birthplace of King Henry V. William FitzOsbern had a motte and bailey here near the junction of the Monnow and the Wye. In 1272 the fortified bridge was built and its impressive gate tower, the only one of its kind in Britain. It dates from the end of the thirteenth century when Monmouth was a walled town.

In 1673, the Duke of Beaufort built Great Castle House, demolishing much of the castle to do so. It has been an Assize Court, a girls' school and today it is the Regimental Museum of the Royal Monmouthshire Royal Engineers.

(RMRE) Open 1 April – October 3.00 p.m. to 5.00 p.m. Use town car park.

80. Monmouth

THE THREE CASTLES

The Three Castles Grosmont, Skenfrith and White Castle are all around 5 miles from each other in a large triangle. They were brought into one ownership by King Stephen in 1138. They were administered by the Sheriff of Herefordshire so that the area between the River Wye and the Black Mountains could be kept under Crown control. The Welsh raiders were a constant menace and one sheriff was killed at Dingestow (a few miles south of Skenfrith) in 1182. Ralph of Grosmont was a military engineer who strengthened all three castles at this time. King John granted all three castles to Hubert de Burgh and later Hugh acquired Montgomery, Cardigan and Carmarthan castles.

94. GROSMONT

Grosmont is a much securer castle than Skenfrith with a strong gatehouse, large hall area, strong corner towers, a deep moat and bank beyond. There is evidence that, like Goodrich, this castle was adapted for more luxurious living in less troubled times.

95. SKENFRITH

Skenfrith lies close to the River Monnow as the river filled the moat. It is a polygonal shape with corner round towers and a circular keep. Waleran, the German who was constable of the three, built a chapel at Skenfrith. In 1241, a receipt survives showing that crossbows and quarrels were purchased from St Briavels Castle where they were made as well as wax for the chapel candles and pans for the three kitchens. In 1254, Prince Edward was given the castles but he passed them to the Earl of Lancaster and they remained Crown property.

CADW and NT. Open all daylight hours (Tel 01874 625515).

Right: 81. Grosmont chimney

Below: 82. White

96. WHITE CASTLE

Isolated on a hill off the Skenfrith to Abergavenny Road, White Castle is built with soldiers in mind. It has a huge thirteenth-century outer ward with large walls where an army could camp and a further bailey on the other side or hornwork, also surrounded by the moat. Pevsner suggests that the Sheriff of Herefordshire paid £128.16s on this castle between 1184 and 1186. The other improvements took place in the thirteenth century when Llewelyn ap Gruffud was threatening the area. The last governor of the three castles was John Morgan, whose tomb is in Skenfrith church, dated 1557. After a brief period of private ownership, the three castles are in the hands of CADW.

Open daylight hours.

FOREST OF DEAN

97. ST BRIAVELS

In the Forest of Dean stands the impressive small castle of Milo Fitz Walter, which has a massive gatehouse. In 1160 it was taken over by Henry II and remained a royal castle, used especially by King John for hunting in the forest. Here was the constable warden of the forest's headquarters and what is the chapel today used to be the courtroom. There is an oubliette in the east drum tower and the keep no longer exists but stood at the back of the small bailey.

King Edward I used the castle as a factory and store for crossbow bolts made in the forest by iron founders and used by his castle garrisons. They also shaped stones for large catapults and trebuchets.

Today, having been a prison, St Briavels is a youth hostel and the royal bedroom is full of bunk beds; King John would not be happy.

EH. Bailey open April – September, 1.00 p.m. – 4.00 p.m. The interior room open once a year in September. Tel: 01594 530872.

83. St Briavels front

84. St Briavels walls

Right: 85. St Briavels entrance

Below: 86. St Briavels King's House

CHESHIRE

98. ALDFORD

On Blobb Hill the De Aldfords had a castle built to defend a ford over the Dee.

99. BEESTON

Situated close to Tarporley, south of Chester, Beeston Castle stands on a 740-foot-high isolated rock. It was begun by Ranulf de Blundeville, Earl of Chester, in 1222. Ranulf died in 1232 with the castle unfinished, and it was Edward I who finished it in 1303. It has a long climb in a hollow way to reach the outer gatehouse of two D-shaped towers. Further up is the Inner Gatehouse, another two D-shaped towers and a long walkway, but no sign today of any living quarters. Only a few rubble walls remain of the curtain wall, but in most places the steep descent would have kept attackers out.

During the Civil War it was held by a small devoted band of Royalists and only surrendered in November 1645. The Chester Parliamentarians commanded the civilians of all neighbouring villages like Tarporley to slight the castle, which was done most effectively. The grounds are a favourite picnic spot. The view covers eight counties and nearby Peckforton Castle, which is a nineteenth-century private house.

EHT Open Feb – March weekends 10.00 a.m. to 4.00 p.m., April – September 10.00 a.m. to 6.00 p.m., October – November, 10.00 a.m. to 5.00 p.m., November – 15 February 10.00 a.m. to 4.00 p.m. Telephone 01244 402111 for further details.

100. CHESTER CASTLE AND TOWN WALLS

Chester Castle today has all but vanished. The Roman town had a Norman castle built by William I's cousin, Hugh Lupus. Today the only thing that remains of it

87. Beeston

88. Chester walls

is part of the high walls and the Agricola Tower, which contains a chapel and a regimental museum.

Chester was a Palatinate, that is, it controlled its own defence against Welsh attackers and enjoyed special privileges. In 1237, it became a royal possession. The Northern Marches were controlled from Chester and it built its own courtrooms, prison and other necessary rooms for local government.

The city walls, started by the Romans, cover 2 miles and are kept in remarkable condition. The locals and tourists use them regularly and some of the towers are kept in equally good condition – the best is King Charles' Tower. Here in the Civil War, King Charles I watched his troops being beaten at Rowton Heath in September 1645. The Governor, Sir Nicholas Byron, refused to surrender the city until food ran out in February 1646. The walls were repaired and Thomas Harrison completely rebuilt the castle area, adding barracks, between 1792 and 1810.

City walls open at all times. King Charles' Tower has a Civil War exhibition. Chester Castle, Agricola Tower and old castle walls, including chapel open for guided tour groups only. Can be booked online. Telephone 01244 972120 for details.

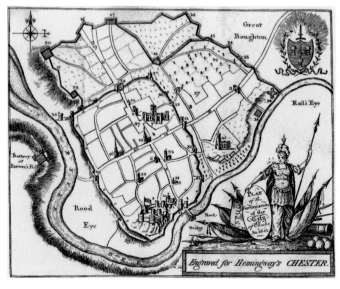

89. Chester plan

101. DODDINGTON

A tower in Doddington Park, south of Crewe, marks the site of Poitiers hero, Sir John Delves', fortified mansion. Freestanding, it has stone knights representing Delves, Fowlehurst, Hawstone and Dutton, who at one stage in the battle defended Sir James Audley's small force against an attack by 300 French cavalry.

102. DODLESTON

The moated site of the Boydel's Castle can be seen near the Flint border. It was the headquarters of Sir William Brereton during the Civil War siege of Chester.

103. DUNHAM MASSEY

Hamo de Masei had a castle here. All that can be seen today is the lake which was constructed out of the moat.

NT property near Altrincham open to the public. It has a café and shop.

104 FRODSHAM

On Overton Hill near Runcorn are the remains of Frodsham Castle, a home of the Earls of Chester. In 1654 it was destroyed by fire and a Mr Ashley built a new house incorporating the castle cellars.

105. HALTON

A Henry II castle on a high hill belonging to the De Lacy family stood here. It was used by John of Gaunt as a hunting lodge. Destroyed after the Civil War, when it was held by Lord Rivers for the king, some of the walls remain but the gatehouse is now a pub and a ruin nearby is an eye-catcher to improve the view from Norton priory.

106. MACCLESFIELD

Castle Field is all that remains of the site of another castle of the Earls of Chester.

107. MALPAS

A large motte near the church is the site of a castle to keep out the Welsh. It also belonged to the Earl of Chester.

108. PULFORD

On the Wrexham to Chester road near the River Alyn, the Pulfords built a castle to defend the area against Owain Glyndwr's rising. Sir Thomas Grosvenor set out with his Cheshire men from here to defend the Marches.

109. SHIPBROOK

Richard Vernon had a castle near Northwich on Castle Hill which was still there at the end of the seventeenth century.

110. SHOCKLACH

Only earthworks remain now of a castle on the Dee. It was the property of Lord Dudley in Elizabethan times, then the Corbets of Stoke and finally the Breretons during the Civil War. If you look carefully inside the church (key with a local farmer) there is a carving of a man with a spear on a horse; he looks more Saxon than Norman.

111. SHOTWICK

A stronghold of Ranulf de Blundeville on the Wirral, this was once an important castle with a polygonal tower. Troops went from here to Ireland in the thirteenth century and its owners were Stanleys, Egertons and Breretons.

112. STOCKPORT

Close to the church stood the castle of Geoffrey de Costentin built, probably on a Roman site, during the reign of King Henry II.

NORTH WALES

113. CHIRK

The massive castle here, south of the Dee, was begun around 1282 by Roger Mortimer. He probably based it on an earlier work dating from a marcher stronghold in Henry II's reign believed to have been built by a Welsh prince, Jorwerth the Red. It is a large square courtyard building with four drum towers in each corner and a middle tower on the north front. There are no signs of baileys or outer ditches or walls. It became the property of the Myddletons in 1595. Sir Thomas Myddleton was a wealthy merchant and Lord Mayor of London. In the Civil War, the owner had to attack his own home without damaging it as it was taken by the Royalists. Cromwell certainly damaged it in 1645 when it surrendered, but it has been well looked-after by the Myddletons with various improvements to the interior by Pugin and the chapel by Blomfield so that it has become a star attraction of the National Trust, since 1981, with much to see both inside and outside.

NT Open all year (Telephone 01691 77701 for details.) Car park (not in shade), shop and restaurant. Open Bank Holidays.

114. DENBIGH

Denbigh in Welsh is 'Dinbych' or a small fort. There is nothing small about this castle. Edward I in 1282 took over a Welsh structure built by Dafydd ap Gruffudd and gave this new castle to the Earl of Lincoln, who became the Marcher Lord for this area. Owners after this seemed to lose their lives frequently. Henry Lincoln's son Edmund fell into the castle well, the younger son fell off Pontefract battlements. Thomas, Earl of Lancaster, lasted eleven years but was beheaded for treason and so too were Hugh Despenser, favourite of Edward II (1322) and Roger Mortimer (1330) then finally Henry IV gave it to Hotspur Percy, who was killed when rebelling against King Henry at the Battle of Shrewsbury (1403). Jasper Tudor

90. Chirk

91. Denbigh

burnt the town and a new town had to be built. It passed briefly to Robert Dudley, Queen Elizabeth's favourite, and during the Civil War it was held by the Royalists under William Salisbury of Rug. Finally, it was surrendered to Gen. Mytton in October 1646. The castle then became robbed of stone until it was briefly repaired in Victorian times and turned over to Cadw. It has seven towers and an unusual gatehouse of three towers. The town wall abuts the Red Tower.

The castle is best approached by foot up the steep footpath (indicated by a large green key close to 'Boots'). Motorists are advised to drive up to the car park on the far side of the town.

CADW. Open during daylight hours. Shop and ticket office. Car park off Love and Castle Lanes. Pedestrian approach via Broomhill Lane.

115. FLINT CASTLE

Substantial remains can be seen on Edward I's first castle, which stands close to the Dee Estuary. Started in 1277, it was supervised by James of St George, the main builder of Edward's castles. The inner bailey is square with three round corner towers but the fourth tower or keep is separated by its own moat with a drawbridge to reach the inner bailey. At 23 feet thick, this great tower has accommodation, a chapel and storage space. Here Richard II awaited Henry Bolingbroke. In Shakespeare's words, 'Down, down I come like glistering Paethon ... Down court, down King.' Richard was taken to London and forced to abdicate. In the Civil War, it was surrendered to Parliament and in 1652 it was 'slighted' (demolished).

In 1944, J. Goronwy Edwards, a Fellow of the British Academy, gave a lecture there on 'Edward I's castle building in Wales' in which he stressed the huge labour force that came from all over England to build the castle – carpenters, masons, smiths, ditch-diggers and even charcoal burners – so that the costs were high in wages: Flint cost £7,021.13s.7¾ between 1277 and 1286 and, most workers then going on to Rhuddlan, the amount there was even more: £9,505.15s.9¼p. How he managed to dig up these figures in the middle of the Second World War I do not know!

CADW. Open at all times. No ticket office or shop.

116. RHUDDLAN

The original castle here in North Flintshire was the home of Gruffyd ap Llywelyn, but was destroyed by Harold Godwinsson in 1063. The original motte and bailey was turned into the impressive ruin you see today, built by Richard of Chester and by Edward's master mason, James of St George.

It has the Clwyd River on the south-west and a moat round three sides. The garrison could be supplied by sea. There were two wards – the inner with two towers and impressive twin-towered gatehouses at east and west corners.

Above: 92. Flint

Left: 94. Rhuddlan interior

Unlike Chirk, the towers had four storeys. The royal chambers, chapel and kitchen, probably all timber-framed, have vanished. The town gate has a pit for a turning bridge. The outer ward had a tower defending the dock. During the Civil War, it was captured by Col Mytton for Parliament. The diamond-shaped inner ward had two entrances and the moat was narrow so defence must have been difficult. Fortunately, compared with Denbigh and Flint, much of Rhuddlan remains.

CADW. Open during daylight hours. Ticket office and shop. Maisy's café recommended nearby.

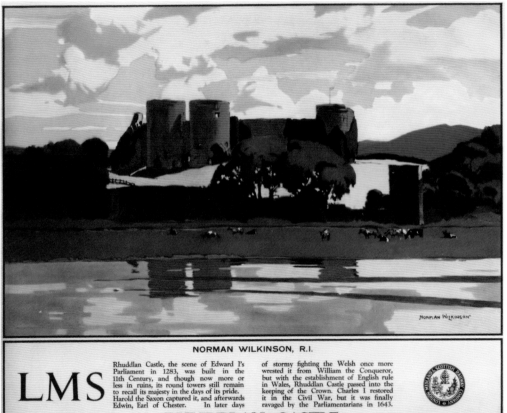

NORMAN WILKINSON, R.I.

LMS

Rhuddlan Castle, the scene of Edward I's Parliament in 1283, was built in the 11th Century, and though now more or less in ruins, its round towers still remain to recall its majesty in the days of its pride. Harold the Saxon captured it, and afterwards Edwin, Earl of Chester. In later days of stormy fighting the Welsh once more wrested it from William the Conqueror, but with the establishment of English rule in Wales, Rhuddlan Castle passed into the keeping of the Crown. Charles I restored it in the Civil War, but it was finally ravaged by the Parliamentarians in 1643.

RHUDDLAN CASTLE

93. Rhuddlan Castle

LIST OF ILLUSTRATIONS

79.   Montgomery (Oman)
80.   Monmouth (CSOT)
81.   Grosmont (Oman)
82.   White Castle (Oman)
83.   St Briavels, front towers (CSOT)
84.   St Briavels, walls (CSOT)
85.   St Briavels, entrance (CSOT)
86.   St Briavels, King's house (CSOT)
87.   Beeston from the air (English Heritage Trust)
88.   Chester walls (English Heritage Trust)
89.   Chester, Hemingway map of walls & castle
90.   Chirk Castle (Royal Commission on the Ancient and
       Historical Monuments of Wales)
91.   Denbigh Castle (author)
92.   Flint Castle keep (author)
93.   Rhuddlan Castle by K.Wilkinson (York Railway Museum)
94.   Rhuddlan interior (author)

Appendix – The Mortimers of Wigmore Castle

1. Ralph
Hastings veteran, remained loyal to William I, was given forfeited manors of Wigmore, Cleobury and Bridgnorth. Died 1104.
2. Hugh
Opposed Henry II and was deprived of Bridgnorth Castle. Founded Wigmore Abbey 1181.
3. Roger
Occupied with fighting the Welsh. Died 1215.
4. Hugh
Supported King John. Died 1227.
5. Ralph
Brother of Hugh. Fought the Welsh. Married Black Gladys, daughter of Llewellyn the Great.
6. Roger
Friend of Henry III. Planned escape of Prince Edward. Commanded rearguard at Battle of Evesham and his men killed Simon de Montfort. Married Maud de Braose. Their third son, Roger, was builder of Chirk Castle.
7. Edmund
Married Margaret de Finnes, relation of Queen Eleanor of Castile. Died 1304.
8. Roger.
Married Joan de Geneville, wealthy lady who brought him Ludlow Castle. Rebelled against the King but was captured and sent to the Tower of London. Escaped to France where he became friendly with Queen Isabella. Died as a traitor in 1330 at Tyburn.
9. Edmund
Lived peacefully.
10. Roger
Married Phillipa, daughter of 1st Earl of Salisbury. Fought at Crecy. Earl of March. Was restored to all Mortimer lands after his grandfather's attainder in 1355. Lived at Ludlow Castle and died 1360.

11. Edmund, 3rd Earl of March

Married another Phillipa, daughter of Lionel, Duke of Clarence. Became Earl of Ulster and a claimant for the Crown. Their daughter, Elizabeth, married Harry Hotspur. Edmund died 1381.

12. Roger

Married Eleanor Holland, niece of Richard II. Heir to throne in 1385 but died in local Irish war in 1398. Buried at Wigmore Abbey.

13. Edmund

Aged ten when Henry Bolingbroke seized power from Richard II. Made a Royal ward with his young brother Roger. The latter died young but Edmund fought with Henry V. Died 1424. The king founded a chantry to the two brothers at Chichester Cathedral.

14. Anne

Sister to Edmund and Roger. Married Richard Plantagenet, Earl of Cambridge, grandson of Edward III. Their son Richard, Duke of York, was killed at the Battle of Wakefield, 31 December 1460. Young Edward, Earl of March and his brother Richard were still there to carry on the Yorkist struggle with Lancaster that ended when Edward IV died and Richard became King Richard III. The Battle of Bosworth, August 1485, saw the death of Richard III and the victory of Henry Richmond, who founded the Tudor dynasty as King Henry VII.

Notes above are printed with kind permission of Edmund Vale, author of *Shropshire* in the County Book series.

GLOSSARY

Bailey	A castle enclosure, defended by earth banks and palisades, later replaced by walls of stone.
Barbican	A sloping part of a castle wall, often defended by a battery.
Belfry	A defensive outwork, often protecting the main gate as at Goodrich.
Berm	A narrow flat space outside a wall, which could be used as a postern for troops to go left or right.
Brattice	A wooden platform built out from battlements, often given machicolations in the floor for dropping items on attackers.
Chantry	A chapel built (often in a cathedral) for priests to say prayers for the deceased. A useful source of income for the building.
Crenellate	To add a battlemented parapet to a house, making it defensible by archers or crossbow-men. A licence was required from the sovereign before this could be done.
Drake	A small cannon, around 6 lb, common in the Civil War as easily transported by a horse or several men.
Drum Tower	A flat-topped circular tower (as at Chirk Castle).
D-Shaped Tower	A castle tower flat on one side and curved on the other.
Garderobe	A latrine, usually next to a wall.
Halberd (or Halbert)	A long wooden weapon with a spike or hook on one end or short axe. It was common in the fifteenth and sixteenth centuries, and in the eighteenth century it was used by sergeants, often for getting men into line.
Juliet	A circular donjon (as at Flint Castle).
Keep	The most heavily defended tower in a castle. In France, a donjon (dungeon is the same word but has a different meaning). A shell-keep is usually circular with rooms inside and a sentry path around the roof.

Machiocolation	A hole in the brattice for pouring boiling boiling oil on attackers, usually between portcullises.
Mangonel	A siege engine used for slinging medium-sized stones.
Oubliette	A bottle-shaped dungeon where the prisoner was thrown in and forgotten (see St Briavels).
Quarrel	A short square-headed (metal pointed) arrow for a crossbow. Some were made at St Briavels in the Forest of Dean because of the availability of iron there.
Slight	To destroy a castle, usually by gunpowder or cannon, to render it unusable for potential enemies. Bridgnorth Castle is a good example.
Trebuchet	A siege-engine that operated by counter-poise. It is believed to have been invented by the Romans.

Bibliography

Acton, Mrs F. S., *The Castles and Old Mansions of Shropshire 1142–1660*

Crossley, F. H., *Cheshire* (Hale, 1949)

Duncombe's *History of Hereford, Vols I – V* (Evans & Jeffries, Pall Mall, London, 1804)

Edwards, J. Goronwy, *Edward I's Castle Building in Wales* (British Academy Rhŷs Lecture 1944)

Evans, L., *The Castles of Wales* (Constable, 1998)

Fletcher, H. L.V., *Herefordshire* (Hale, 1948)

Forrest, H. E, *Some Old Shropshire Houses & Their Owners* (privately published, 1924)

Fry, P, Somerset, *The David and Charles Book of Castles* (1980)

Kinross, J., *Discovering Castles in England and Wales* (Shire, 1973)

Kinross, J., *Houses with Private Chapels in the Heart of England* (Fineleaf Editions, 2010)

Mais, S. P. B., *Highways and Byways in the Welsh Marches* (Macmillan, 1939)

Mee, Arthur, *The King's England:*
  Herefordshire (1938)
  Cheshire (1968)
  Monmouthshire (1951)
  Shropshire (1950)

Moss, Fletcher, *Pilgrimages to Old Houses* (Published by the author, Didsbury, 1903)

Oman, C., *Castles*, (Great Western Railway, 1926)

Pettifer, A., *English Castles* (Boydell Press, Woodbridge, 1995)

Pevsner, *The Buildings of England:*

Pevsner, N & Brooks A *Herefordshire* (London, 2012)

Pevsner, N & Newman, J., *Shropshire* (London, 2006)

Pevsner, N., Hartwell, C., Hyde, M., & Hubbard E., *Cheshire* (London, 2011)

Philips, Alan, *Castles and Fortifications of Wales* (Amberley, 2011)

Pye & Lillistone *Guidebook to Lyonshall Church & Castle*

RCHME, *Herefordshire* (Vols I, II & III H M Stationery Office, 1934)

Renn, D, *Norman Castles* (John Baker, Humanities Press, 1968)

Robinson, Revd C. J., *A History of the Castles of Herefordshire* Logaston Press, Herefordshire, 2002.

Rowley, T., *The Welsh Border* (Stroud, 2001)

Salter, M., *Castles of Gwent, Glamorgan & Gower* (Folly Publications 2002)

Salter, M., *Castles of Herefordshire & Worcestershire* (Folly Publications 1989)

Salter, M., *Castles of Shropshire* (Folly Publications 2001)

Shoesmith, R, *Castles & Moated Sites of Herefordshire* (Logaston Press, 2009)

Victoria County Histories: Hereford & Shropshire

Tewkesbury Battlefield Society, *The Street Banners of Tewkesbury* (2013)

Vale, E, *Shropshire*, (Hale, 1949)

Webb, Revd T. W., *Memorials of the Civil War in Herefordshire* (1879, Kingsthorn reprint, 2002)

Wright, T., *History and Antiquities of Ludlow* (Rev.edtn. Morten, 1972)

INDEX